LIVE INSPIRED

LIVE INSPIRED! The young person's introduction to Emotional Intelligence and the pursuit of purposeful goals

This book may be purchased for business or promotional use or for special sales. For information, please email info@ks4inspiration.com

Book design by Albatross Book Co.
Edited by Carmen Riot Smith
Initial Logo Design by Farzana Abedin

ISBN 978-1-7376458-0-1

www.KS4Inspiration.com

THE YOUNG PERSON'S INTRODUCTION
TO **EMOTIONAL INTELLIGENCE**
AND THE PURSUIT OF PURPOSEFUL GOALS

KEVIN R. SAUNDERS

For Isaiah, Noah, Isaaci, Isani, Julianna, Marcel, Christian, Alyssa, Max, Ace and the ones to come.

For Mom.

CONTENTS

INTRODUCTION

Live Inspired – To be in active pursuit of goals aligned with your purpose.

Emotional Intelligence (EQ) – The capacity to blend thinking and feeling to make optimal decisions.

There may come a time in your life when you feel empty, confused, and lost. I felt that way as a teen making the transition from high school to college, as a college graduate trying to figure out how I would make a difference in the world, and as a young man starting a family and wondering how I would help my children make sense of the world. I pondered timeless questions:

"What am I here for?"

"What is my purpose here?"

"What is my contribution?"

I'm writing this book because I want you to begin the questioning stage sooner than later so that you can start making decisions and taking actions in agreement with your purpose. I am encouraging you to *live inspired*!

To live inspired means that you are in active pursuit of goals aligned with your purpose. When you live inspired you are intrinsically motivated to work toward something greater than yourself. You are energized because you know your life is valuable and your time on this earth means something.

But what is that "something"? If you already have your answer to this key question, that's great! You're a step ahead of most of us! For those of us still searching and evaluating what's real to us, I'm here to help. This is my contribution to your journey of self-discovery.

To keep it all the way real, I don't expect that your questioning stage will end today, tomorrow, or by the time you finish reading this book. The reality is that even if you think you have your answers . . . your answers require confirmation. And nothing will confirm your true purpose like life experience. It's the trials and tribulations of life that will challenge you and sometimes discourage you. But if you press on, you will overcome these trials and they will empower you and shape your perspective and values. If you truly engage in this self-study, you will not only learn to align your actions with your purpose, but you will also equip yourself with tools to help you navigate the emotions that come with life challenges.

There are obstacles in any road worth traveling. Whether you are a high school student struggling to envision your future successful self, a college student who is second guessing your chosen field of study, a young professional or entrepreneur who is realizing that there is more to life than money, or a parent/educator who wants to put some pep in the step of the next generation, a little inspiration may be all you need to start moving intentionally toward your purpose. Maybe you get the point by now and you already appreciate the message. Or maybe you're wondering whether you can trust the messenger?

Why listen to me? Well, let me help you get familiar.

My name is Kevin Saunders and I have been placed on this earth to inspire others to live purposefully. I'm passionate about making a positive impact on the youth, specifically middle school, high school, and college students, as well as young professionals and entrepreneurs who are ready to make their contributions to the world. I am the creator of KS4Inspiration, which provides inspiration and education to the next generation so that our young people will have the knowledge, discernment, and confidence required to achieve meaningful and impactful goals.

I would describe myself as a creative and driven young black man who has achieved some career success in the face of societal and personal obstacles. I am married to my amazing wife Jennifer and we have two of the best boys in the world, Isaiah and Noah. I graduated from Pace University with an MBA in accounting and I am currently a senior manager at Deloitte, a global professional services firm. I am a Certified Public

Accountant (CPA), a Certified Financial Planner (CFP), a spoken word poet, and a certified emotional intelligence (EQ) practitioner. Above all else, I am an encourager who just wants to help! If you don't know, now you know!

The impact I've made in the lives of others is evidence of my faith in God and is only possible thanks to the support of my family and many other talented, determined, and compassionate individuals who have supported and encouraged me in my purpose. These people challenged me to further develop my God-given attributes, to push the boundaries of what I thought was possible, and to persevere through adversity. They helped me recognize that I have something to offer this world. They challenged my perspectives and expanded my view of what is possible. It is time for me to pay it forward. Please allow me to be a voice of encouragement for you. Cool?

Alright then, let's get right to it! In order to live inspired you need to know what's important to you, set goals that are meaningful, explore pathways to achieve your goals, commit to your success, and believe that you can do it! To help you envision what your inspired life looks like, I ask you to think critically about your response to the following key questions:

5 Key Questions to Live Inspired:

- What is the intersection of your passion, purpose, and talent?
- What are your goals?
- What are the pathways to achieving your goals?
- Are you willing to commit to achieving your goals?
- Do you believe that you can achieve your goals?

At the end of each chapter you will identify a key takeaway from what you learned. Don't skip this part! You will need a key takeaway from each chapter to construct your fun and creative self-reflection at the end of your journey. Your self-reflection is your master plan, your own personal guide to living inspired!

Your ability to identify and navigate your emotions is a vital element of your inspired life. How will you respond to feelings of frustration, disappointment, and regret that may arise when things don't go according to plan? How do you address feeling overwhelmed and stressed on your road of success? Are you able to overcome feelings of jealousy, self-centeredness, and fear in order to build authentic and healthy personal and professional relationships? Your emotions can dictate your response to life circumstances for the better or for the worse.

Emotional intelligence is the capacity to blend thinking and feeling to make optimal decisions. As you go through each chapter, you'll learn about EQ through the lens of the Six Seconds EQ model. Six Seconds is a nonprofit organization that is dedicated to supporting people creating a positive change. They offer EQ training, certifications, and resources in countless countries and numerous, professional, academic, and social settings. Their EQ model focuses on three important pursuits and encourages the development of eight key EQ competencies.

3 Pursuits of the Six Seconds EQ Model

- Know Yourself – Clearly see what you feel and do (self-awareness)
- Choose Yourself – Do what you mean to do (self-management)
- Give Yourself – Do it for a reason (self-direction)

The Six Seconds EQ Model		
Pursuit	**Competency**	**Definition**
Know Yourself	Enhance Emotional Literacy	Accurately identifying and interpreting both simple and compound feelings
	Recognize Patterns	Acknowledging frequently recurring reactions and behavior
Choose Yourself	Apply Consequential Thinking	Evaluating the costs and benefits of your choices
	Navigate Emotions	Assessing, harnessing, and transforming emotions as a strategic resource
	Engage Intrinsic Motivation	Gaining energy from personal values and commitments versus being driven by external forces
	Exercise Optimism	Taking a proactive perspective of hope and possibility
Give Yourself	Increase Empathy	Recognizing and appropriately responding to emotions
	Pursue Noble Goals	Connecting your daily choices with your overarching sense of purpose.

To KNOW YOURSELF is to be self-aware. When you know yourself, you can clearly see what you feel and do. Are you able to identify your emotions and recognize your patterns of response?

To CHOOSE YOURSELF is to practice self-management. When you choose yourself, you do what you mean to do. Are you able to evaluate the costs and benefits of your choices? Are you able to navigate your emotions, using them as a strategic resource? Are you intrinsically motivated or are you driven by external forces? Do you exercise optimism, transforming hope and possibility to solutions and options?

To GIVE YOURSELF is to have a sense of self-direction. When you give yourself, you do things for a reason. Do you pursue meaningful goals and take actions that are aligned with your purpose? Are you empathetic to yourself and others?

These are the key competencies you will develop as you build the foundation of your EQ skills. At the end of each chapter, I will challenge you to practice EQ and take action in real time in order to accelerate your development. If Allen Iverson needs to practice, then you do too! If you don't get that joke, hit YouTube. Anyway, enough of the hype and suspense. It's about to go down! It's time for you to focus on yourself. I'm excited to walk with you on this journey of self-discovery. Ain't nothing to it but to do it! It's time to live inspired!

By the end of this journey you will:

- Live Inspired! Practice EQ skills with engaging and interactive learning experiences
- Set goals aligned with your talents, passions and purpose
- Explore the job and career pathways available to achieve your goals
- Navigate your emotions in order to overcome obstacles and remain committed to your goals
- Build self-confidence and exercise self-compassion
- Identify national and local community partners that can provide educational and recreational opportunities for continued engagement

List of Emotions

Practice EQ - What emotion do you feel as you begin a journey of self-discovery that may impact the rest of your life?

Peaceful	Sad	Mad	Scared
Content	Apathetic	Angry	Anxious
Loving	Ashamed	Critical	Confused
Nurturing	Depressed	Distant	Discouraged
Pensive	Grief	Frustrated	Embarrassed
Relaxed	Guilty	Hateful	Fearful
Responsive	Inferior	Hurt	Helpless
Secure	Isolated	Jealous	Insecure
Serene	Lonely	Sarcastic	Insignificant
Thankful	Remorseful	Selfish	Overwhelmed
Trusting	Sleepy	Skeptical	Pessimistic

Joyful	Powerful	Energized
Amused	Ambitious	Determined
Cheerful	Appreciated	Focused
Creative	Bold	Healthy
Daring	Confident	Inspired
Energetic	Faithful	Invigorated
Excited	Optimistic	Motivated
Fascinating	Proud	Refreshed
Hopeful	Respected	Renewed
Optimistic	Surprised	Strengthened
Playful	Valuable	Vibrant

Refer to this short list of emotions throughout this study to expand your emotional vocabulary.

ONE

What is the intersection of your passion, purpose, and talent?

So you want to be a doctor, huh? Why? You want to save lives? Why? Why do you feel a life is worth saving? Is there another way to save lives that would feel satisfying to you? What has influenced your desire to become a doctor? Is it money? Power? Respect? Do you love helping people? Do you dislike seeing others suffering? Or do you want to be an educator who teaches about the medical field? What is motivating you toward this goal? Maybe you have a gift for paying attention to detail? Is there a specific person you would like to heal? Are you truly passionate about being a doctor? Is it part of your purpose for being? You aren't sure, are you? Is this your first time thinking critically about this? If so, that's ok, you're not alone! Let's dig deeper.

Passion

Passion – Any powerful or compelling emotion or feeling, as love or hate.[1]

I never felt as excited and enthused to dive into a project as I was to create music and produce an album. As I pondered the reason why I enjoyed it, I found that it was not just that I enjoyed listening to my own songs, but I loved making other people think. As I continued to explore different artistic expressions, my experiences led me to finding my talent for using my words, actions, and creativity to positively impact others. I absolutely LOVE this.

I knew I was passionate about it because I felt alive and filled with joy not only when my creation was complete, but also in the process of creating! The word passion directly refers to your emotions—what you're feeling. Passion is not a single emotion but refers to the level of intensity that the emotion is felt.

> **You are within the proximity of your passion whenever you feel *energized in the process* of what you're doing!**

It can be an activity or hobby such as stand-up comedy, writing short stories, building robots, painting, or photography. After close self-examination, you may also find that there is minimal emotional connection to the activities you do. You may find that you don't have something that you're passionate about . . . yet. *That is okay!*

In that case, I challenge you to get outside and get involved! You likely just need more exposure to different experiences. Start by considering extracurricular or recreational activities offered by your school, organization, or local community center. Even if you discover that you're not interested in a particular activity, that's still valuable information! You're one step closer to finding something that truly moves you. Don't stop . . . keep going! Keep trying different things until your passion begins to reveal itself in the form of energy and enthusiasm.

Is there an activity or hobby that you have that you always look forward to? What is it about that activity that energizes you?

Describe an activity or hobby that you've tried and disliked. What is it about the activity that drained you of your energy?

You can also be *energized by a challenge that you're facing or something that you want to change*. For example, in 2015 while in the sixth grade, Marley Dias started a book drive intended to make sure that more young black girls like herself would see themselves represented in books. She started the campaign #1000blackgirlbooks and as a result she was able to collect more than eight thousand books to donate to young girls. Since then she has gone on to publish an activism guide for children and teens with reputable educational publisher Scholastic.[2]

Marley didn't need to search far and wide for a cause to champion. She felt that her experiences as a young black girl were not represented in the books she was reading. She undoubtedly felt overlooked and undervalued. These strong and unpleasant emotions are a form of energy! Young Marley decided to use that energy to make a positive impact for herself and for others that may be feeling the same thing.

Is there a problem or challenge you have encountered in your life that needs to be addressed? Is there something that makes you say

"someone should do something about this"? Well, guess what? That someone is you. You are who you have been waiting on.

Maybe there is a cause you would like to support? Or a group of people you would like to help? You may feel energized volunteering at a homeless shelter, adopting a dog, coaching a youth soccer team, raising awareness for fair voting rights, donating toys to sick children in the hospital, or—in my case—sharing inspirational poetry with the youth.

The desire to solve a problem that impacts you or others is another energizer that can lead you to your passion. To identify potential causes that move you, start by thinking critically about life challenges that affect you and the people you love. Then consider the different ways (big and small) that you may be able to help them and others that may be going through the same thing. For example, if my uncle has lung cancer due to his lifelong smoking habit, I may come up with a big plan to cure lung cancer. Awesome! I may also start an anti-smoking campaign at my school/organization to warn my peers about the dangers of smoking. Outstanding!

Is there a cause you would like to support or a group of people that you would like to help? Specifically, what can you do to provide support?

Emotions are indicators of what matters to you. As you become more in tune with what you're feeling, clarity in the *what*, *why*, and *how* of your life will follow. You will need to effectively navigate your emotions in order to harness that energy and do amazing things! EQ skills are necessary because we need to understand how our emotions affect our response to the challenges we face. Throughout this study you will engage in activities designed to enhance your EQ skills. If you're feeling confused, uncertain, or overwhelmed as you think about these things (maybe for the first time), that's okay! That is an appropriate response when dealing with personally and emotionally complex subject matter. Yet and still, I encourage you to *keep going!* Be patient with the process of growth and self-discovery.

The Key to Passion:

- Passion – any powerful or compelling emotion or feeling, as love or hate.
- You are within the proximity of your passion whenever you feel energized in the process of what you're doing!
- Your passion may lie in an area of study or an activity that you enjoy. Get out there and try new things.
- You may be passionate about helping yourself and others overcome a challenge. Thinking critically about life challenges that affect you and the people you love. Consider different ways (big and small) that you may be able to help them and others that may be going through the same thing.
- Live in your passion and give it your best. With time and experience, allow yourself to reassess whether you remain energized by it.

Purpose

Purpose

1. *(noun) The reason for which something exists or is done, made, used, etc.*
2. *(verb) To set as an aim, intention, or goal for oneself.*[3]

If passion is the "what," then purpose is the "why." And the "why" is deep! I'm not going to ask you existential questions like "why are you here" or "what is the reason that you exist?" My intent is to have you consider whether you *would like* your life to have meaning. To decide that your life has meaning is to place value on who you are, who you will become, and what you do. To decide that your life is valuable requires an answer to the question "in what way do I add value?" What is my role on this earth? In my community? My classroom, my peer group, my family, my church, mosque, or temple? Since you're reading these words, I'll assume that you feel that your life has meaning and that you add value. I don't expect you to discover your purpose by the end of this chapter. It may not reveal itself for quite some time. But until it does, let's begin our exploration of purpose by understanding the connection between our belief set and our purpose.

In the United States, we are each entitled to our own beliefs, but in certain settings it is still considered taboo to talk about the morals, values, and faith that set the foundation for one's character—the ideals that guide our daily decisions consciously and subconsciously. Society is more willing to talk freely and openly about sex, drugs, and rock n' roll, yet we're expected to stay far away from sharing our morals, values, and faith. But guess what? We ain't running!

As we begin to share with others what matters most to us, it is important that we respect our peers and accept the fact that others may have a different belief system. According to a 2015 Pew Research Center study, 84% of the global population identifies with a religious group.[4] In encouraging you to explore your purpose, you must clear a path in your journey to reflect on how your faith factors into your decisions. For many of us, our faith is the guiding force behind how we aspire to live our lives, how we treat others, and the goals that we ultimately pursue. For instance, as a Christian, I believe that we are born in a specific place, with unique personalities and talents (gifts) in order to fulfill our mission on earth of loving God and loving others. As an adolescent, I lived out my faith when I did community service events, such as serving food at a soup kitchen, or participating in the March of Dimes fundraiser for premature babies.

In what ways do you actively live out your faith?

I know there are some rock stars out there that do things like this because they find it personally fulfilling and want to do something great for others. But I must confess that I did these things in my younger days because my parents encouraged me to do it or my school required it. The initial motivation to participate was not from within, but the act of helping others in need still brought me joy. It provided evidence that even little old me has something to offer. I discovered that helping others was its own reward. Thus, as I grew older I found myself looking for different ways to help. My faith was instilled in me by my parents and it plays a big part in who I am and how I view my purpose. Serving others led me to experiencing the inherent joy that comes along with that. I eventually became intrinsically motivated to help others in many ways. If you too are a person of faith, consider the role your faith plays in your life.

What does your faith teach you about your purpose in life?

Intrinsic Motivation

> *Intrinsic motivation – Engaging in a behavior because it is personally rewarding; essentially, performing an activity for its own sake rather than the desire for some external reward.* [5]

I asked you twenty-one questions at the onset of this chapter because you won't find your "why" at the surface level. You will need to go deeper than extrinsic or tangible rewards in order to uncover it. During the early part of my professional career, I learned just how important the EQ competency of engaging intrinsic motivation is to living inspired.

For many years, I worked within a career path that drained me of my natural energy and optimism. Upon graduating from Pace University with both my bachelor's and master's degrees in business administration with a focus in accounting, I received an offer from Morgan Stanley to work as an HR generalist, and another offer from Deloitte Tax as an entry-level tax consultant. I decided to continue down the path my degree had taken me and accepted Deloitte's offer, beginning my career in tax accounting, preparing and reviewing tax returns. The primary driving factor for the decision was long-term financial reward. The prospects of greater career growth and bigger financial rewards down the line was more enticing to a young and ambitious Kevin. I was trying to get paid!

I didn't see too much of a difference between the two options because both would help me achieve my personal goals. A personal goal of mine at that time was to live a nice lifestyle. Having gone through college borrowing meal cards from freshman, walking around in old clothes, and riding around in a beat up 1999 Kia Sephia (R.I.P.), I wanted to look and feel like I achieved some success. Living at home with my parents after graduating just didn't scream to the world that I made it. I wanted to own a home, drive a nice car, wear some designer clothes, and be able to stunt a little bit among my friends. So my immediate concern was getting a good job that could help me do these things. Looking back, I don't understand why I was surprised that I was something less than captivated by my career choice. I didn't really choose the career . . . the career chose me. What I chose was the money. I was extrinsically motivated. I likely would have embarked on almost any legal career that offered the least resistance and would take me there fastest.

So there I was, sitting at a desk trying to become an expert in something I had zero interest in. I was trying to become a leader in a field that I found boring and somewhat arbitrary. I was able to get promoted from staff to senior consultant, and obtain the Certified Public Accountant (CPA) designation, but I did this on the strength of my test-taking aptitude and ambition. Yes, I passed the exams. Yes, I was promoted to senior. Yes, these accomplishments provided temporary happiness, or rather relief that I was able to live up to my own expectations. But the passion for my professional career was lacking. I didn't look forward to going to work. I didn't feel that my work made a positive impact on anyone. I knew I could be the best tax consultant in the world if I applied myself. But why would I put so much effort into work that didn't mean much to me or the people I was working with?

Describe a time when you felt like what you were doing didn't matter to you or anyone else.

As I continued to go through the motions in my career, I found myself looking for external distractions to make my laissez-faire ride to the top of my firm bearable. I created a flag football league, I got lost in the world of fantasy football, I created expansive music playlists for every occasion, and I was always on the scene with the homies at bars and clubs. I was one thousand times more engaged and interested in these activities than my daily grind at work.

I'm sure you get the point by now. I had no passion for the work that I was doing. There was only an obligation to do the work to obtain the monetary reward that I truly desired. I was extrinsically motivated by money, power, and status. Obtaining the reward was my motivation; it was my "why." There was no greater meaning or purpose behind the early career decisions I made. You don't have to travel down the same unfulfilled path.

Describe your motivations for achieving academic and/ or professional success. Are your motivations intrinsic or extrinsic?

Even as I made my money-driven decisions, I knew deep down that my purpose was to make a positive impact in my community. My purpose was first revealed to me during my college days when I had the pleasure of serving as a resident assistant and President of the Black Student Union at Pace University. My experience helping my fellow students make new friends on campus and encouraging them to explore activities that interested them only confirmed my earlier inclinations that my purpose is tied to serving others. Said another way, further experience confirmed that I am intrinsically motivated to serve others. I serve because it feels good to help someone else. For me, serving others is its own reward. The direct and indirect positive impact in someone else's life energizes me. It is my why!

Describe an instance when you took action that resulted in a positive impact in your life or someone else's life.

What has your life experiences confirmed or revealed about your intrinsic and extrinsic motivations?

As you continue to explore and consider your purpose, I urge you to look beyond the extrinsic rewards and truly focus on what is internally rewarding. I'm not saying that money isn't a thing! It is an important tool that we need to live our lives, and a powerful resource that can be used to make a great impact in our surrounding environment. It is a necessary tool to escape the grip of poverty that plague so many in this nation, especially people of color. What I am saying is that money isn't THE thing!

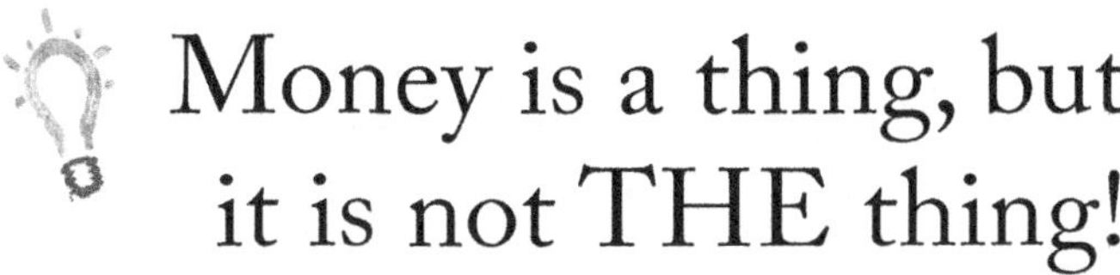

Chasing money for money's sake can lead you astray of your purpose and your mission, if it is not appropriately prioritized. Yes, there can still be financial reward on the path to fulfilling your purpose. If living a certain lifestyle is part of your personal goals, *that's ok, that's REAL!* But when you ponder your purpose, ask yourself, what would you do *AFTER* you have achieved your lifestyle goals. What is the point of it all?

Imagine that you won the lottery and all of your lifestyle goals were instantly achieved. What would you do with your financial freedom? What would you do with the rest of your life? Why?

Is there a way for you to do what you've written above without winning the lottery? Have others done it without being rich or wealthy?

Now that you've spent some time examining your purpose, let's consider how your passion, purpose, and talent may be interconnected. We can spend more time at the intersection of passion, purpose, and talent if we're willing to open our minds and be a little creative. We all have talents within us that need to be nurtured and developed. Let's continue our discussion with the exploration of our talents.

Talent

Talent – A special natural ability or aptitude.[6]

If passion is the "what" and purpose is the "why," then your talents and gifts are the "how."

It is easier to succeed at something that you're passionate about. Even if you are missing the skill set that typically accompanies your passion, if you're truly passionate about something, you're more willing to dedicate yourself to learning about it. You're more apt to commit to your own success and work through obstacles that arise. Michael Jordan loved basketball, he wanted to be the best to ever play the game. He wasn't always the GOAT (greatest of all time). He didn't make his high school varsity basketball team during his sophomore year in high school.[7] But his passion for the game allowed him to overcome that disappointment, and continue to work on his craft. Eventually, he persevered. His commitment to his passion along with his gift of natural athletic ability led to his success as a player. More important than his financial rewards, his success as a player positioned him to be a source of inspiration for people all around the world.

Becoming the best at anything will be difficult. It will take immense work and commitment. Reaching the highest of heights becomes that much more difficult when you're uninspired, or when you're only motivated by external reward such as money or fame.

If your objective is to receive a tangible reward, you will entertain many different pathways to achieve it. If one pathway is too strenuous, you'll look for a path of lesser resistance, with little regard as to whether that path is meant for you to walk. You'll just blindly follow a path to what you think you want, rather than moving intentionally toward the path you were meant to walk.

Are you motivated to become one of "the best" at anything? If so, what and why?

Michael Jordan's story is proof that we can expand on our base talent level to become a greater version of ourselves if we are willing to commit to the work required to do so. Yet, his story deters some of us from doing just that. Why? Because many of us haven't identified the talents that we have. We haven't identified the thing that we're uniquely good at or a passion that we're willing to invest in. We think that our talent needs to be ready-made. Meaning you either have it or you don't. But that's far from the truth! We're not identifying our talents because when we start our search for it as young people, our talents are typically in their infancy, not fully developed. To make matters worse, we compare our beginning talent level to legends who have invested blood, sweat, and tears nurturing their talent for years on end. We need to remember that Michael Jordan at age fourteen was not the same Michael Jordan who won his first NBA championship at age twenty-eight.

Stop discouraging yourself by comparing yourself to the greats. Instead, compare yourself from yesterday to today and be encouraged by your own growth!

I promise you, your talent is in there somewhere! It's waiting on you to find it, believe in it, and maximize it to the fullest. The best way for your talent to reveal itself is for you to try different activities and challenge yourself. This is one reason why participating in extracurricular activities are so important. So go ahead and take pictures for the yearbook, write for the school paper, join the art club, debate team, entrepreneurs society, or soccer team. Each experience will bring new ideas and perspectives, help you develop new skills, and determine whether there is a talent that is calling you to commit to its development.

Identify one or two of your talents that you would like to nurture and develop.

The Intersection of Passion, Purpose, and Talent

Early in my professional career, I realized that the further I strayed from my purpose by prioritizing rich man ambitions, the more I began to resent my caviar dreams and Lamborghini nightmares. I began to truly examine the factors driving my decisions. Once it became clear that my priorities were out of line, I made an adjustment. I began to seek my purpose within my chosen career. I could've just quit my job and become a full-time musician, but that wasn't realistic in that moment given my responsibility to provide for my wife and son. So I pivoted and found a way to positively impact others by becoming a financial planner within my company.

I chose financial planning because I became passionate about the prospect of attaining financial freedom and teaching others how to do the same. My role as a financial planner allows me to help others develop a plan to achieve their financial goals, which means that I get to spend most of my career working hours living in my purpose by making a positive impact. Also, over the years I nurtured my talent for organizing information and communicating clearly and effectively. These are skills that I get to use on a regular basis as I present a financial plan to a client one-on-one or deliver a presentation to over five hundred of the firm's national leaders live on stage in Las Vegas.

To live inspired is to spend as much time as possible at the intersection of talent, passion, and purpose. For example, if you're a talented singer and you have an innate need to help children, the intersection of talent, passion, and purpose would be to teach elementary school music. Doing so would inject meaning into your day. You would be enthused and excited to go to work. You would not be going through the motions. If being an elementary school music teacher doesn't allow you to live the lifestyle you hope for, then perhaps you can go pro and produce or perform music that appeals to children. If you have the outward personality and desire to be a famous pop star, you can certainly go that route. But if you're more of an introvert, maybe you can work behind the scenes writing or singing for children's cartoons and television shows. So we won't just sing to make money so we can donate to children's charities. If that were the case we could be tempted to sing about anything, even if our music is harmful to those we want to impact positively. We will make our songs about uplifting and caring for children. We will teach children the skills that we possess. That's the intersection!

But what happens when circumstances are beyond your control and building a career directly within your passion and purpose isn't possible? What if you're not in the financial position to move on from that passionless job? Then you choose your attitude!

You infuse meaning into your days and hours by focusing on the positives of your role while taking note of the duties of your

role that drain you. You gather as much data as you can about the elements of your role that you like and dislike, and you take advantage of opportunities to invest in yourself while in that role.

You adapt and try to infuse as much purpose as possible into what you're doing. We waste no time!

Consider how your experience in your role can be used to live in your purpose. Maybe there are people that you are meant to help or that are meant to help you in some way. All experience is useful and will help you in making your next move your best move. If you can navigate your emotions successfully by choosing the right attitude, then you can uncover information that is valuable to your journey of self-discovery even in the most challenging situations.

The point is, no matter your personality, or talent, or current situation, you can choose to live inspired and find a way to walk in your purpose. You don't have to compartmentalize how we make our living from our purpose for living. These two things can be connected, so it's up to us to marry them so that we can live an inspired life. Doing so will require some creativity, individual questioning, and mindfulness/prayer. The first step to living inspired is to STOP and THINK! So let's do it.

What is the intersection between your talent, passion, and purpose?

In closing, it is the activities and causes that you are passionate about that can help you identify your "why." If you can apply your talents to live in your passion and purpose in some way within your career, you will avoid spending most of your waking hours doing tasks you can't stand just to gain external rewards that provide temporal happiness. Your intrinsic motivations are signals that can lead you to your purpose, your "why." Knowing your "why" will help guide your steps so that you can make academic, career, and life decisions that will allow you to live inspired and make decisions that are in line with your purpose. To find your purpose, dig into the area of your passions, specifically where they intersect with your talent. Grab your shovels, let's go!

Practice EQ

1. Apply Consequential Thinking — Increase Self-Awareness and Accepting Feedback
   a. Your educators, mentors, friends, and family may see something in you that you can't or are unwilling to see. Identify two to three people that know you and that *you truly trust*, and ask them the below questions about yourself. Don't be deterred if they disagree with your assessment of yourself. Whether right or wrong, their statements will put you in a position to either accept or challenge their assessment, leading you closer to recognizing the true you.
      i. When do you notice that I am most excited?
      ii. What do I talk about the most?
      iii. What talents do I possess?
      iv. What are my three strongest characteristics?
      v. How can I make a positive impact in my community in my own unique way?

2. Navigate Emotions — Practice Mindfulness
    a. Analyzing our lives can be a stressful and emotional experience. It's important that you're armed with EQ tools and best practices to help you on your journey of self-examination. One tool that can help is mindfulness. Many studies show that practicing mindfulness reduces stress, decreases emotional reactivity, and enhances self-insight, morality, and intuition.[8] So set your body in the most relaxed posture possible, start to breathe slowly, clear your mind of cluttered thought, and allow yourself to just be present. If this is your first time practicing mindfulness, please visit the KS4Inspiration YouTube channel for a mindfulness demonstration.
3. **Engage Intrinsic Motivation – Key Takeaway #1**
    a. Now that you're in a clearer state of mind, in your personal notes, write down your response to the following questions. If you're not quite ready to answer the questions, write down the emotions that are triggered by each question and consider why you may be having that emotional response.
        i. What are your talents?
        ii. What are you passionate about?
        iii. What have your life experiences taught you about your purpose?
        iv. What career or academic pathway would allow you to use your talents within your passion in service of your purpose?

Notes

Notes

Notes

TWO

What are your goals?

Define Your Success

Success — The accomplishment of an aim or purpose.[9]

What does the word success mean to you? Success is a relative term. Based on the messages we receive consciously and unconsciously, I wouldn't blame you if your definition of success included elements of wealth, fame, or power (WFP, pronounced "wefp"). Our problem is that we let society define success for us. If it's not our parents, relatives, or friends, then it's television, movies, social media, and music. As much as I enjoy the more conscious hip hop out there, the more authentic and vulnerable songs don't get much airplay. When I turn on the radio all I hear is "I got 1, 2, 3, 4, 5, 6, 7, 8 M's in my bank account."[10]

My intention is not to define *your* success, but to help you avoid being so basic. I want to encourage you to set purposeful goals that go beyond WFP and instead focus on living inspired. WFP in and of itself is not evil. Each element should be viewed as a resource to make positive change in society. Each can be the result of making a positive impact. After completing chapter 1, you have a fundamental understanding of the word purpose, even if you're not quite sure what your personal purpose may be. The word "success" is defined as the accomplishment of an aim or purpose. Connecting the dots, we should recognize the process of pursuing our purposeful goals as success, instead of the potential byproducts that come along with achieving them.

For example, Kevin Hart, one of the greatest comedians in the world today, is successful because he consistently executes his goal of making people laugh. The WFP that comes after years of learning, making mistakes, investing in his talent, and committing to his goal is a byproduct of his success; it is not success itself. If you can start to appreciate that success is in the process of pursuing a goal, and not the resulting byproduct of the goal, you're one step closer to achieving true success.

Real success becomes attainable when you commit to the process, the craft, the work! Once you've executed and achieved your goal, surrender the outcome, knowing that WFP and other extrinsic rewards are not promised.

Just ask the talented rapper whose YouTube video will never hit one million streams, or the state senator that lost her reelection bid by ten votes, or the NASA astronaut who didn't get her shot to walk on the moon.

The present danger is that most of society commonly defines success and one's value by their WFP.

> If we measure our value by WFP, we will seek these things incessantly since they will be inextricably tied to our self-worth. Please know that your value is in your character and integrity. Your value lies in how you treat others. Your value is in the positive impact you make in your community, now and in the future.

I define my success as living in my purpose, loving God and loving others, fulfilling His mission for me of inspiring and encouraging others. I am actively succeeding in my mission as I am executing my vision, encouraging the youth via spoken word poetry and inspirational workshops. Many have told me that they are inspired by my poetry, videos, and workshops. Some just can't relate. Their response is out of my control. It took me some time, but I'm finally cool with that. WFP may or may not come from my efforts . . . and I'm cool with that too. I'm loving the process, the craft, the work, and I'm committed to executing the vision! So I can let the chips fall where they may. My success is not dependent on becoming wealthy, powerful, or famous. Is yours?

I define success as...

Pursue a Noble Goal

The most successful businesses have one overarching goal or reason for being in business, beyond just making profits. They have a mission statement that keeps them focused on their purpose and their value to the world. Here are some mission statements from a few highly successful businesses. The most critical decisions made and strategies executed by a business are in harmony with their mission statement. When a strategy or proposed action is in direct conflict, they stay clear. Here are a few examples of company mission statements:

Nike: Bring inspiration and innovation to every athlete in the world. *If you have a body, you are an athlete.*[11]

Patagonia: Build the best product, cause no unnecessary harm, use business to inspire and implement solutions to the environmental crisis.[12]

Tesla: To accelerate the world's transition to sustainable energy.[13]

Red Cross: The American Red Cross prevents and alleviates

human suffering in the face of emergencies by mobilizing the power of volunteers and the generosity of donors.[14]

KS4Inspiration: Provide inspiration and education to the next generation so that our young people will have the knowledge, discernment, and confidence required to achieve meaningful and impactful goals.

Daily decisions are evaluated through the lens of the mission statement to ensure the business doesn't chase a desired outcome at the expense of its values. For example, Tesla is in business to make money, but their mission to accelerate the world's transition to sustainable energy cautions them from seeking profits from the production of gas guzzling vehicles which are harmful to the environment. Because their mission is to transition the world to sustainable energy, they make electric rechargeable vehicles instead.

Let's take the concept of a company's mission statement and make it personal. How does this apply to you?

Your purpose is not a destination, but it is the navigation system that helps you determine the right paths to take in your ongoing journey.

Without a navigation system, we can easily be led astray of our purpose and lose ourselves to the traps of the world. Creating your own personal mission statement, or "noble goal" as it's referred to in the Six

Seconds world, will help you navigate through the twists, turns, ups, and downs of life and ultimately continue to live inspired, walking down your purposeful path.

A key competency of the Six Seconds EQ Model is "Pursuing Noble Goals." A noble goal is a brief and compelling statement of purpose that helps you evaluate your choices. It is intended to help you "connect your daily choices with your overarching sense of purpose."[15] A noble goal meets the following criteria:

- Not complete in your lifetime – It is enduring and inspiring, something beyond the daily struggle. This helps you maintain a long-term focus so you can avoid the confusion of short-term thinking.
  Ex. The Red Cross alone will not be able to end human suffering. But their noble goal provides clarity on what they are working toward every day.
- Pointed outward – While you will benefit, the focus is on others. This helps you maintain an expansive vision.
  Ex. Inspiring and educating others is the focus of KS4Inspiration, and yes, I am energized (intrinsic) and financially compensated (extrinsic) for it.
- Integrates different domains – It encompasses all dimensions of your life; work, family, community, and spirit.
  Ex. My personal noble goal is "to inspire others to live purposefully." I can live this noble goal at home by encouraging my family, at church by sharing my testimony, at work in conversations with clients, etc. It instructs my behavior in the different areas and relationships in my life.
- Gets you out of bed – It motivates and inspires you at a deep level; it helps you to have the energy when the going gets tough.
  Ex. You look forward to living in your noble goal. It is a passion, a source of energy for you.

- No one made less – No one has to be "less than" or "wrong" for you to pursue your noble goal; this helps you stay out of ego and power struggle.[16]

    Ex. If I want to "inspire others to live purposefully," I can not also commit to "proving the doubters and haters wrong."

Elements of a Noble Goal:

1. **Not complete in your lifetime** – It is enduring and inspiring, something beyond the daily struggle.
2. **Pointed outward** – While you will benefit, the focus is on others.
3. **Integrates different domains** – It encompasses all dimensions of your life; work, family, community, and spirit.
4. **Gets you out of bed** – It motivates and inspires you at a deep level; this helps you to have the energy when the going gets tough.
5. **No one made less** – No one has to be "less than" or "wrong" for you to pursue your Noble Goal

Each of these criteria are important, but the most powerful one in my view is that a noble goal should be focused on the benefit of others. If your success is somehow tied into helping or benefiting others, you will receive an internal reward that will create a sense of satisfaction and gratitude. You don't have to take my word for it . . . His Holiness the Dalai Lama and Archbishop Desmond Tutu come to the same conclusion in their interfaith conversation as documented in the *Book of Joy*.[17] Two well-known spiritual leaders, one a Buddhist monk and the other a follower of Christ, both conclude that loving and helping others is a key component of living joyfully in the human experience. Successfully living in your noble goal will be more fulfilling and will bring joy if it is focused outward! I absolutely love and appreciate this element of creating a noble goal because my experiences serving the youth via KS4Inspiration and serving the community via my church have confirmed that this is true. I receive more energy and more life each time I have an opportunity to share my experiences in order to help others. The act of serving others is powerful.

Now that you know the criteria used to construct a noble goal, give it a shot! In chapter 1, you began the process of identifying your passion and purpose. All you have to do is use the criteria above to reframe your passion and purpose into a powerful noble goal in the space below. Don't worry about having a perfect noble goal on your first try. You will have additional opportunities to refine and reassess your noble goal as you continue your journey of self-examination. As you begin to live inspired and learn more about your passion and purpose, things will become clearer. As you have new life experiences, new relationships, and new environments, you will notice that your values and perspectives may begin to grow and change. Likewise, you will need to allow your noble goal to grow and change with you. With the future uncertain, all you can do at this moment is focus on what is important and meaningful to the person you are today. So let's do it!

 **What is your Noble Goal?**

SMART Goals

SMART goal – A goal that is specific, measurable, achievable, realistic, and time-based.

Why is it important that you set goals? So that you're working toward something. When you created your noble goal, you identified that "something." You now have a north star to help guide your decision-making and lead you to living an inspired life. You can now focus on setting SMART goals, the destinations we aspire to reach as we live within our noble goal. After all, a pilot doesn't fly an aircraft without knowing where he is going to land. In 1981, George Doran first articulated that we should work to ensure that our goals are specific, measurable, assignable, realistic, and time-related.[18] Since then, other scholars, including Professor Robert S. Rubin, have revised and expanded upon the SMART criteria as follows:

Elements of a SMART Goal:

- Specific
- Measurable
- Achievable
- Realistic
- Time-based

Specific and Measurable

Goals need to be specific and measurable so that we can assess our progress to our goals. Those that do set goals are often too vague, saying "I want to be a multi-platinum musician." First of all, the goal can be more specific. Are you a pop singer or a drummer in a band? Ariana Grande or Questlove? Do you want to have one album go 2x platinum or would you be happy going 2x platinum over your entire music career? Being specific firms up your vision, making it more real.

Achievable and Realistic

Goals need to be achievable so we can be motivated to achieve them. Nothing kills motivation like being asked to do the impossible.

If you set a goal to be loved by every human on planet earth, you will give up by the time your extended family gets together for Thanksgiving dinner . . . and that's *your family*! Goals that are dependent on results are not always within our control. To ensure that your goal is achievable, focus on what is within *your* power. Instead of "being loved by every human on planet earth," focus on "kindly greeting each new person that I meet." Goals are meant to be challenging! Creating achievable and realistic goals is not a license for you to dream small, to take it easy, or to be satisfied with minimal progress in your development.

To set a realistic goal is to know where you want to go, to understand where you are today, and to be able to envision a pathway to achieve it.

In the present moment, you may not have the financial resources, connections, knowledge, or skills required to achieve the goal, but if you know that you are capable of learning, growing, and adapting to life's circumstances, then you can remain encouraged that the goal is realistic and within reach. So yes, "becoming the CEO of a fortune 500 company" or "walking on the surface of Mars" are both realistic goals. To make them achievable goals, you would reframe the goal to be within your power (i.e. "I need to develop my leadership skills by sharing and discussing knowledge articles with my colleagues monthly," and "I need to practice the Mars landing simulation and get a perfect score on the final exam."

Time-based

The most effective written goals are time-sensitive. Without an element of time, your goal is open-ended and will live longer than you do! We want to outlive our goals, conquering them one by one in order to make room for the next new and exciting challenge.

That's why we use time constraints. Instead of thinking of time as pressure, consider it a motivator to get after your goal and take action today! Having time-based goals also helps you prioritize your efforts today. Having a goal of "graduating from Columbia University with a bachelor's degree in psychology" can be completed in four years or eight years if you go part-time. It can be completed by age twenty-three or age sixty-three. The element of time makes your goal more specific, measurable, achievable, and realistic. If you would rather not have the pressure of a looming deadline, think of time as part of the goal instead of the completion point. For example, "I will spend two hours per day reading a new book" or "I will have Saturday brunch with my best friends once a month."

The SMART criteria is just a framework for making your goals more actionable. Don't stress yourself out trying to apply each criteria to every single goal, because it may not be applicable in all cases. The reason we're discussing the criteria is so you can be specific and add clarity to your vision of what it means to live inspired. With a clearer vision of where you need to go, you can carefully assess the feasibility of different pathways to get there. We'll discuss pathways to achieve your goals in chapter 3.

What is one personal, professional, recreational, or academic goal that you currently have?

Rewrite the above goal to make it Specific, Measurable, Achievable, Realistic, and Time-based (as applicable).

Respect The Process

Goals can deter you. The grander the goal the more likely we are to doubt our ability to achieve the goal. That's because there is a certain amount of investment in our skills and abilities that's required in order to reach a level of exceptionalism so that we can attain the goal. In his book *Outliers*, Malcolm Gladwell states that it takes ten thousand hours for one to truly become an expert at something. Just hearing ten thousand hours of work is enough to dissuade most people from starting on the road to pursuing their goals. We see the work that's required and the skills that we need and we immediately doubt whether we can achieve the goal because our future successful selves look nothing like who we are today.

My future successful self is disciplined, has eliminated distractions like video games and club-hopping, he is confident, and in touch with the needs of his community, he is an expert in his field, and a world-renowned artist who has positively impacted the human experience through writing, art, poetry, speaking, and music. That future self is intimidating, not encouraging! Live in the present and focus on taking one step toward becoming that future self each day. The hours, days, months, and years will pass faster than you can imagine. Focus on what can be done TODAY to keep moving forward. Set goals for tomorrow, take action today.

Goals are aspirational. A goal is a destination you hope to arrive at. The importance of the goal is the personal development and growth that comes during the process. A music artist who sets a goal of "winning a Grammy for Best New Artist" must understand that they are not in control of the votes that will determine the winner. The artist is in control of the creative process, the hours spent practicing, and the marketing of their music. With some goals the outcome is not always promised, so surrender the outcome and commit to the process. Don't travel the road *to* success . . . it takes too long to get there and the destination lasts for a moment. Instead take the road *of* success that acknowledges your personal growth and development in each step on the way to your destination. I encourage you to break your lofty goals into goals focused on the process instead of a particular outcome that may be out of your hands. Setting SMART goals is about having checkpoints where you can continually assess your progress toward your aspirational goals and determine whether you're on the right track, living inspired.

Why is it a good idea to focus on achieving SMART goals?

How are SMART Goals connected to your Noble Goal?

With each SMART goal you achieve, you build confidence and momentum. When a challenging goal is accomplished you further your belief in the skill of self-discipline and your ability to overcome obstacles. Furthermore, you build momentum by directly applying that boost of confidence to the next challenging goal. In the process of achieving each goal, we take several steps toward our future successful selves. By recognizing our growth and the achievement of our goals we encourage ourselves to do better, do more, and go harder! I KNOW you have the ability to achieve your goals. I KNOW that if you invest in yourself and commit to the process that you will arrive at your desired destination. But once you know what you want to accomplish, you have to start with the crucial first step of your journey . . . writing your goals down!

The first step to achieving your goal is to make your aspiration real by writing down your goals. A study conducted by Dr. Gail Matthews, a psychology professor at the Dominican University in California, revealed that those who wrote down their goals and dreams on a regular basis achieved their aspirations at a significantly higher level than those who did not. The study also found that those who communicated their progress to a supportive friend achieved their goals significantly more than those who had only written out their goals, had unwritten goals, or who formulated action commitments.[19] The bottom line is that:

If you want to increase the odds of achieving your goals, write them down to make them real, and then share your progress with an encouraging person.

What could feel more amazing than bringing your vision to life? To set your mind and heart on something, take action, and make it real? Each time I bring my ideas and perspectives to life in the form of a spoken word poem I feel joyful, excited, humble, proud, sometimes sad, but always present and connected to my audience. So, I can tell you that to live out your vision is to live inspired. And for you, it starts now with step one: write it down and make it real!

Practice EQ

1. **Pursue Noble Goals - Key Takeaway #2**
   a. What is your noble goal?
      i. Develop a concise noble goal based on the noble goal criteria. Extra credit if you can condense it into just six words or less. For example, using my definition of success as a starting point, I summarized my noble goal into one easy-to-remember sentence: "To inspire others to live purposefully."
2. Apply Consequential Thinking – What are your SMART goals?
   a. To the best of your ability, create at least one goal in each of the following areas as applicable:
      i. Academic
      ii. Professional
      iii. Financial
      iv. Extracurricular or Hobby
      v. Personal growth
      vi. Spiritual growth
      vii. Physical fitness
      viii. Mental and emotional Health
   b. We need to make the above goals SMART and focused on the process to increase the likelihood of achieving them. Ask the

following questions of your goals and rewrite each of them to apply the SMART criteria as needed.

i. Can I make this goal more specific and measurable? Or is it so specific that it is limiting or restrictive?

i. Is the goal dependent on others? What portion of this goal is within my control? How can I make this goal dependent on my actions only?

i. Is the goal too easy or is it impossible?

i. Is this goal time-sensitive? Should it be? Is my time frame even possible?

c. Are your SMART goals in line with your noble goals? Try to find a direct or indirect connection to your noble goal. If it is not connected in any way, consider whether it is a goal worth achieving.

d. *For the uncertain: If you aren't sure what your passion is, it will be difficult to set goals, let alone work toward them when obstacles arise. In your case, consider setting goals to try a new activity each month, or learn something new about a point of interest every week. Your issue may be a lack of exposure to options of who your future successful-self CAN be.

3. Increase Optimism – Team Me & Team You
   a. Identify supportive classmates, coworkers, friends, or relatives who you feel comfortable sharing your progress toward achieving your goals. Invite two or three people to join "Team (your name)." If they agree to join your team, communicate with them how they can most effectively support you.
   b. Don't stop there, encourage your team to achieve their goals as well! Ask them how you can most effectively support them and commit to checking in with each other on a regular basis.

Notes

Notes

THREE

What are the pathways to achieving your goals?

With most goals there is more than one pathway to achieving it. That's why it's important that you explore the different paths available to advance you forward. One reason we struggle with achieving our goals is that we don't know which route to take to get there. Even if we do have an idea of how to get there, we're usually aware of only one or two paths to success. We may see someone else in a position that we aspire to be in and assume that we just need to follow in their footsteps to get to a similar place. We don't consider the fact that this person has different talents, motivations, and characteristics which would make the path they chose perfect for them, but likely daunting for you. There are many routes to the same destination. Find yours.

For example, my noble goal is to inspire others to live purposefully. There are many ways I can achieve this. I can write a best-selling book, have a meaningful conversation with a close friend, write an inspirational poem, or make viral YouTube videos. These are different means to the same end, which is to inspire.

The question is, what path shall I take? The answer is . . . the one best suited for me.

Part I – Explore
Explore & Know More

Exploration Day is one of the programs KS4Inspiration conducts specifically for middle and high school students. The program encourages students to explore different career paths and helps them connect their long-term goals to the decisions that they make today. Professionals in different fields—ranging from architecture to medicine, fitness, and business—make themselves available to students to paint a picture of what it means to work in their roles. The down-to-earth, real talk, and major keys shared by the professionals is always well-received and appreciated by the students. For many of them, the session is an introduction to careers or entrepreneurial pathways they never knew existed. So they not only learn of opportunities that are out there in the world, but they begin to envision opportunities that they can create and trails that they can blaze!

Some students may lack exposure to different career paths and opportunities because they never visually "see" anyone in the role. This is especially true in minority communities, where our children's imaginations for what they can be is limited to what they see and experience in their own homes and neighborhoods, or what they consume via TV, music, and social media. There is not a broad range of women and minorities in different fields being shown in our national media, which is why movies like *Hidden Figures* (black women scientists), *Concussion* (black doctor), and *Zero Dark Thirty* (lead female investigator) can have such a subconscious impact on what our youth view as possible for themselves. If you are someone with a limited imagination of what you can become and the heights you can reach, this chapter is especially for you! It's time to open your mind and see what's possible!

Career Map

What follows is a career cluster map which summarizes different careers based on a particular area of interest. Review each career path and consider which specific career pathways you would like to learn more about.

FOUNDATION KNOWLEDGE AND SKILLS

Academic & Technical Skills // Teamwork // Problem Solving

Emotional Intelligence

Critical Thinking // Ethics // Communication

NATURE PATH

AGRICULTURE, FOOD & NATURAL RESOURCES

- ✓ Agribusiness Systems
- ✓ Animal Systems
- ✓ Food Product & Processing Systems
- ✓ Natural Resources & Environmental Service Systems
- ✓ Power, Structural & Technical Systems
- ✓ Plant Systems

CREATIVE PATH

ARTS, A/V TECHNOLOGY & COMMUNICATIONS

- ✓ Audio/Video Technology & Film
- ✓ Printing Technology
- ✓ Visual Arts
- ✓ Performing Arts
- ✓ Journalism/Broadcasting
- ✓ Social Media Influencer

BUSINESS PATH

BUSINESS, MANAGEMENT & TECHNOLOGY

INFORMATION TECHNOLOGY

- ✓ Network Systems
- ✓ Information Support & Services
- ✓ Web and Digital Communications
- ✓ Programming & Software Development

BUSINESS MANAGEMENT & ADMINISTRATION

- ✓ Human Resources Management
- ✓ Operations Management
- ✓ Administrative Support

MARKETING

- ✓ Marketing Communications
- ✓ Professional Sales
- ✓ Merchandising

FINANCE

- ✓ Securities & Investments
- ✓ Banking Services
- ✓ Accounting

HELPING PATH

HUMAN SERVICES

EDUCATION AND TRAINING

- ✓ Administration & Support
- ✓ Professional Support Services
- ✓ Teaching & Training

GOVERNMENT & PUBLIC ADMINISTRATION

- ✓ Governance
- ✓ National Security
- ✓ Foreign Service

LAW, PUBLIC SAFETY & SECURITY

- ✓ Emergency & Fire Management
- ✓ Law Enforcement
- ✓ Legal Services

HUMAN SERVICES

- ✓ Early Childhood Development
- ✓ Counseling & Mental Health
- ✓ Family and Community Services
- ✓ Personal Care Services

HOSPITALITY & TOURISM

- ✓ Restaurants & Food/Beverage
- ✓ Recreation, Amusement/Attraction
- ✓ Travel/Tourism

BUILDING/FIXING PATH

INDUSTRIAL & ENGINEERING TECHNOLOGY

TRANSPORTATION, DISTRIBUTION & LOGISTICS

- ✓ Warehousing/Distribution Center Operations
- ✓ Facility and Mobile Equipment Maintenance
- ✓ Transportation Systems & Infrastructure Planning, Management and Regulation

SCIENCE, TECHNOLOGY, ENGINEERING & MATHEMATICS

- ✓ Marine Science
- ✓ Astronomy
- ✓ Computer Coding & Programming
- ✓ Environmental Engineering

MANUFACTURING

- ✓ Production
- ✓ Process Development
- ✓ Logistics & Inventory Control

ARCHITECTURE & CONSTRUCTION

- ✓ Design & Pre-construction
- ✓ Construction
- ✓ Maintenance & Operations

HEALTH PATH

HEALTH SERVICES

- ✓ Biotechnology Research and Development
- ✓ Therapeutic Services
- ✓ Diagnostic Services
- ✓ Surgical & Rehabilitative Services
- ✓ Hospital Healthcare provider
- ✓ Nutrition Consulting
- ✓ Communication

Explore Some More

But wait, there's more! You now have a general idea of different career pathways you can take, but what about specific careers within those pathways? The U.S. Bureau of Labor Statistics created the *Occupational Outlook Handbook* tool to provide valuable insight into various career paths. The following is a list of fifty different occupations across the six different career paths.[20] Review the list and answer the questions that follow.

Career Exploration Table		
Occupation	**Entry-Level Education**	**2018 Median Pay**
Athletes and sports competitors	No formal educational credential	$40,000 to $59,999
Bartenders	No formal educational credential	Less than $30,000
Dancers	No formal educational credential	The annual wage is not available.
Models	No formal educational credential	Less than $30,000
Musicians and singers	No formal educational credential	The annual wage is not available.
Waiters and waitresses	No formal educational credential	Less than $30,000
Chefs and head cooks	High school diploma or equivalent	$40,000 to $59,999
Commercial pilots	High school diploma or equivalent	$80,000 or more
Electricians	High school diploma or equivalent	$40,000 to $59,999

Farmers, ranchers, and other agricultural managers	High school diploma or equivalent	$60,000 to $79,999
Photographers	High school diploma or equivalent	$30,000 to $39,999
Plumbers, pipefitters, and steamfitters	High school diploma or equivalent	$40,000 to $59,999
Police and sheriff's patrol officers	High school diploma or equivalent	$60,000 to $79,999
Postal service mail carriers	High school diploma or equivalent	$40,000 to $59,999
Real estate sales agents	High school diploma or equivalent	$40,000 to $59,999
Sales and related workers, all other	High school diploma or equivalent	$30,000 to $39,999
Security guards	High school diploma or equivalent	Less than $30,000
Umpires, referees, and other sports officials	High school diploma or equivalent	Less than $30,000
Actors	Some college - no degree	The annual wage is not available.
Firefighters	Postsecondary nondegree award	$40,000 to $59,999
Hairdressers, hairstylists, and cosmetologists	Postsecondary nondegree award	Less than $30,000
Dental hygienists	Associate's degree	$60,000 to $79,999
Web developers	Associate's degree	$60,000 to $79,999
Accountants and auditors	Bachelor's degree	$60,000 to $79,999

Agents/business managers of artists, performers, and athletes	Bachelor's degree	$60,000 to $79,999
Architectural and engineering managers	Bachelor's degree	$80,000 or more
Clergy	Bachelor's degree	$40,000 to $59,999
Computer programmers	Bachelor's degree	$80,000 or more
Dietitians and nutritionists	Bachelor's degree	$60,000 to $79,999
Environmental engineers	Bachelor's degree	$80,000 or more
Fine artists, including painters, sculptors, and illustrators	Bachelor's degree	$40,000 to $59,999
Personal financial advisors	Bachelor's degree	$80,000 or more
Producers and directors	Bachelor's degree	$60,000 to $79,999
Public relations specialists	Bachelor's degree	$60,000 to $79,999
Registered nurses	Bachelor's degree	$60,000 to $79,999
Writers and authors	Bachelor's degree	$60,000 to $79,999
Zoologists and wildlife biologists	Bachelor's degree	$60,000 to $79,999

Anthropologists and archeologists	Master's degree	$60,000 to $79,999
Education administrators, elementary and secondary school	Master's degree	$80,000 or more
Healthcare social workers	Master's degree	$40,000 to $59,999
Mental health and substance abuse social workers	Master's degree	$40,000 to $59,999
Nurse practitioners	Master's degree	$80,000 or more
Urban and regional planners	Master's degree	$60,000 to $79,999
Astronomers	Doctoral or professional degree	$80,000 or more
Judges, magistrate judges, and magistrates	Doctoral or professional degree	$80,000 or more
Lawyers	Doctoral or professional degree	$80,000 or more
Optometrists	Doctoral or professional degree	$80,000 or more
Pediatricians, general	Doctoral or professional degree	$80,000 or more
Pharmacists	Doctoral or professional degree	$80,000 or more
Psychiatrists	Doctoral or professional degree	$80,000 or more

Source: U.S. Bureau of Labor Statistics

Do any of the careers noted above best suit your talents? Can you connect any of the career paths to your passion and purpose? If so, how?

Are there one or two career paths that you lack interest in? Why do you think these paths may not be for you?

College or Nah?

Whether or not your desired career path requires it, I wholly endorse the college experience. It is a time when you gain more independence, learn the value of self-discipline, meet people from different places and cultures, and expand your worldview. Yes, I have a problem with the current structure of the education system which plummets our youth and their families into deep financial debt, but that's a different story for a different day. If you can find scholarships, work-study programs, or qualify for financial aid to get into a reputable program, I say go for it! Visit www.fastweb.com and www.scholarships.com to kick off your college scholarship search. If you need to commute rather than live on campus to save a few dollars, you should strongly consider it. After you graduate, if you need to live with mom and dad for a few more years while you work, pay down your debt, and save money then do it! Just remember to break them off with a little something each month BEFORE they start asking for a regular rent payment. You'll know you played it right when they're sad to see you move out! That's a pro-tip from someone who's been there.

If you are not interested in continuing your education beyond high school, you have other options. There are many non-traditional pathways where a post-secondary degree is not required. Other pathways may require a certification that you've obtained certain skills or completed a short training program. If those pathways interest you, then find the connection to your purpose and go for it. But the reason I recommend college for all is because receiving an advanced degree expands your career options. There are career paths that you can't effectively pursue without a college degree. Many of the career paths which require an advanced degree eventually lead to higher paying careers and are required for certain leadership roles.

Realistically, we need money in order to provide for ourselves and our families, therefore we must consider this need as we live in our purpose. But we must remember not to let the need drive us AWAY from our purpose.

That's the trap! So I encourage you to pursue a college education in order to expand your horizons and your options. But when it's time to start on your career path, go ahead and get paid! Just don't lose sight of your purpose!

Would you consider obtaining an advanced degree at a college or university? Why or why not?

Entrepreneurship as a pathway

> *Entrepreneur – An individual who creates a new business, bearing most of the risks and enjoying most of the rewards. The process of setting up a business is known as entrepreneurship.*[21]

Remember that your career options are not limited to pathways that currently exist. You may want to create your own cryptocurrency mining farm or create a dating site to help wild ostriches find a suitable mate. You may want to be your own boss and control your own destiny. If you have an entrepreneurial spirit, you can blaze your own trail and start a business that energizes you and is in line with your noble goal. Wouldn't it be great if you were able to spend your workday doing something you love or making a real difference in a cause you're passionate about? Of course, if it were easy to run a business, then everyone would do it! According to the U.S. Bureau of Labor Statistics, approximately 80% of small businesses survive beyond year one, 50% survive up to five years, and only 33% survive for at least ten years.[22] According to a CB Insights survey, the primary reasons new small businesses fail is a lack of demand for the product or service, inability to manage cash flow, inability to form the right support team, and not understanding the competition.[23]

But don't despair! Just because it happened to others doesn't mean it will happen to you. You can learn from their mistakes and you can dig deeper with your research before deciding to go for it. Do the research, learn what it takes to build a successful business, save some money to invest in yourself, connect with some supportive and knowledgeable people, and give it a shot when you're ready! There are all sorts of educational resources to help you along the way. Websites like outschool.com offer exploratory courses to learn more about entrepreneurship. Also, if you're in the United States, the Small Business Administration has some useful information available on their website, SBA.gov.[24] Depending on your location, there may be a Small Business Development Center nearby that can help you start the process of bringing your ideas to life. Your path can be your own!

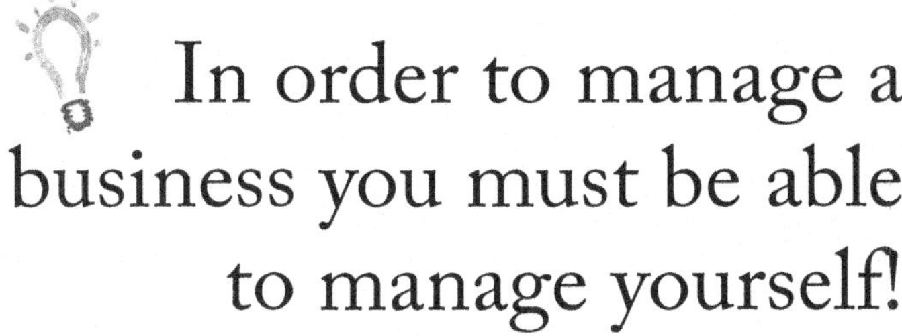

In order to manage a business you must be able to manage yourself!

When you're in charge, there is more at stake. There is pressure to deliver and provide for you and your employees. How will you deal with the emotions that come along with that responsibility? Will you get to a point where you feel overwhelmed and decide to quit and live the statistic? When the money finally starts rolling in and you're feeling on top of the world, will you start spending wildly and living beyond your means? The EQ skills you're developing will help you manage the ups and downs that come along with the sometimes exciting and oftentimes scary journey of being an entrepreneur.

Would you consider exploring entrepreneurial pathways? Why or why not?

You may not feel ready for this today, but as you learn and grow I hope you will at least *consider* entrepreneurship. As I've built KS4Inspiration, I've learned so much about myself and the impact I aspire to make. More than that, my youngest son Noah is beginning to unleash the creator in him. At this moment, he's writing his own book alongside me! It feels amazing to see him start to explore his creativity as he follows my example. The byproduct of your courage in building something is the legacy of knowledge shared with those closest to you. To live inspired is to recognize that sharing our experience for the benefit of others is just as important as the financial incentives we seek.

While we're on the topic, remember, money is a thing, it is not THE thing. It is an important resource but it should not be the sole and primary reason we make career decisions. Think of how a career pathway fits with your talents, personality, passion, and purpose. For more details on various career pathways, download the U.S. Bureau of Labor Statistics' Occupational Outlook Handbook by searching for "CareerInfo" in the App store or Google Play. Dive into the app and let the exploration continue!

Build Emotional Endurance

In finding your pathway to success, knowing what gives you energy is just as important as knowing what drains you. While following your passion, you may find that the experience is not what you thought it would be. It's okay to pivot, or switch lanes once you've had some experience and explored your options. Your experience, whether delightful or dreadful, is valuable information you can use to steer you toward a path better suited for you. I encourage you to be patient when enduring an experience that doesn't immediately meet your expectations. Being uncomfortable is a part of learning. Feeling challenged or stretched in a job or extracurricular activity is not an excuse to cut and run at the first sign of trouble. Your emotions should be considered in deciding whether to continue, but avoid making rash decisions while you are in a highly emotional state.

Your emotions are information. Take heed, but don't let them take control.

Let me give you a very personal example of a time when my emotions affected my career pathway. My oldest son Isaiah was born very premature, about four months earlier than expected. As a result, his lungs were underdeveloped and he regularly developed pneumonia. Very early in his life, there were a few times that my wife Jennifer and I had to rush him to the hospital to make sure he was breathing well. Isaiah is so resilient . . . he always bounced back. However, the reality of his condition weighed heavily on us. I found it increasingly hard to continue to work and provide for us when I was sad, anxious, and concerned about Isaiah's condition. I felt I was letting my team down on those days that I needed to rush to the hospital in the middle of the work day, or call out of work at the last minute. I felt I wasn't doing my best and had become unreliable in a sense.

I was emotionally drained to the point that I decided I needed to resign and focus on Isaiah and Jenn. I called my manager and told her my plan to resign the next day and bring in my laptop. I was done. I felt that I had nothing left to give. When I went into the office and began to say my goodbyes to some teammates, the leader of the team called me in to talk. Long story short, he conveyed that he understood how I was feeling and suggested that I take a leave of absence instead of resigning, just so I could clear my head and focus on my family. In that moment, I realized that I was so in my feelings that I didn't even think of that as an option.

Long story short, that's what I did. Taking a leave of absence allowed me to not only form a plan for my family but also to process my emotions so I could make effective long-term decisions. It allowed me to get paid for a while longer while also maintaining health insurance for Isaiah and avoiding the stress of looking for a new job once Isaiah's condition stabilized. I'm forever thankful for that simple conversation, because that suggested pause allowed the intensity of my emotions to subside, ultimately allowing me to reassess my options and make a better choice. The result was that I was able to be there for my family and still maintain my ability to provide.

Emotions are powerful! We feel frustrated, anxious, sad, disappointed, and stressed at times in life. Sometimes it's personal issues at home that trigger emotions that affect our professional and academic pathways. Sometimes the emotions are triggered by aspects of the pathways we choose. In any case, patience is required to navigate your emotions. You have to allow some time for growth, maturity and understanding.

In fact, I have a wakeup call for some of you: You will not be the CEO of the company or leader of the group or team on day one. You will be in an entry-level position where you will need to take lunch orders, pick up coffee, grab the team bags, wash uniforms, take notes during meetings, make photocopies, load the delivery truck, and clean the bathrooms. Such is life! But if you can navigate your emotions through the ups and downs of the role, there are skills to be uncovered and developed in the process. Skills that you will add to your tool kit and will make you more marketable when you apply for the next opportunity that you seek. Answering the phone is not just answering the phone—it is customer service and conflict resolution skills. Cleaning the bathroom is being a team player. Taking lunch orders is practicing your administration skills—it is an opportunity to expand your network within a company and build your reputation, IF you do it with a positive attitude! It won't be easy, but there is value in it all. Play your role to the best of your ability and get the most you can out of the opportunity. After giving it your best shot, if there is no opportunity to pivot to a different role more suited to you, move on to the next exploratory opportunity knowing that you didn't burn a bridge or harm your reputation. Move on, knowing that you've obtained valuable information about your unique pathway to living inspired.

In life, your ability to persevere will be tested by your emotions; it's just part of the growth and development process. But you are prepared for the test! You're actively learning tools and techniques to manage your emotions and increase your odds of success. Here's one more tool for you:

5 steps to BUILD emotional endurance:

- **B**reathe deeply! It only takes 6 seconds for the intensity of the emotion to subside
- **U**nderstand which emotion you're feeling
- **I**dentify why you're feeling the emotion
- **L**et go of the intensity of the emotion
- **D**ecide on the most appropriate response

When your emotions are running high, take the above five steps to help you navigate your emotions. Let's practice applying the BUILD model to a situation that can trigger a wide range of emotions . . . thinking critically about your future! As you think about your pathway to living inspired, you may feel overwhelmed by all the options you have, you may be excited at the prospect of living in your passion, or you may have feelings of anxiety if no pathway is appealing to you and you don't know where to start. This is an opportunity to BUILD your emotional endurance.

What emotions do you feel as you consider your pathways to living inspired? Use the BUILD model to navigate your emotions.

1) Breathe – Take deep breaths for at least six seconds.

2) Understand – The emotion that I'm feeling is...

3) Identify – The reason I'm feeling this emotion is...

4) Let go – I'm releasing myself from the intensity of the emotion by: stretching, stepping away from the circumstance, talking it through with a friend, exercising, forgiving myself, forgiving someone.

5) Decide – I will respond to the situation by...

Part II - Nothing Confirms Like Experience

Our hopes and dreams are a great source of energy. The vision we create for our lives is beautiful, easy, and enjoyable. But reality is a whole different ball game. You may envision yourself as a family health doctor, cheerfully assessing mom during her annual physical and administering immunizations to her smiling children. But a dose of reality will reveal that a routine physical for mom can become an information session on how to manage her diabetes while her children scream at the top of their lungs at first sight of the vaccination needle. As an optimist, I've found that reality is a distant relative of my grand visions. To bring clarity to your vision for a career pathway, you need experience! You've already done some homework on the different careers that exist and you have identified pathways that interest you. Now it's time to confirm your inclinations with real world experience. Depending on your age and stage of life, you have different opportunities to engage in experiential learning. A few excellent options for experiential learning include: volunteering, hobbies, extracurricular activities, internships, job shadowing, part-time jobs, and mentorships.

Volunteering

Volunteer – A person who performs a service willingly and without pay. [25]

Mahatma Gandhi is widely known as the leader of India's nonviolent independence movement against British rule.[26] Gandhi once said that, "The best way to find yourself is to lose yourself in the service of others."[27] Volunteering is one way you can gain experience in a career pathway and/or discover a cause that is meaningful to you. There are many businesses and organizations that have community programs that require volunteers to execute and drive results. If you are interested in a career in a certain field, you can look for volunteer opportunities within that field to get a better sense of what that career and similar parallel careers truly entail. Your experience volunteering can provide valuable connections with key decision makers in the hiring process, build your self-confidence, yield a sense of purpose, and teach you valuable job skills. Overall, volunteering is an excellent way to invest in yourself! When considering different volunteer opportunities think of the following:

- Would you like to work with adults, children, animals, or remotely from home?
- Do you prefer to work alone or as part of a team?
- Are you better behind the scenes or do you prefer to take a more visible role?
- How much time are you willing to commit?
- What skills can you bring to a volunteer job?
- What skills can you learn from a volunteer job?
- What causes are important to you?[28]

Now let's live it! Consider whether there are volunteer opportunities at your school, at an organization, or within your local community that interest you. To expand your search, visit the following websites and note the volunteer opportunities that interest you:

www.dosomething.org – For youth-led volunteer opportunities.
www.usa.gov/volunteer – Public service and volunteer opportunities for all ages.

List three volunteer opportunities that can help you explore elements of one of your potential career pathways.

Hobbies

Hobby – A hobby is an activity that you enjoy doing in your spare time. [29]

Pro-hobby (productive hobby) – An activity that you enjoy doing in your spare time that produces a skill or explores a profession.

Don't have a passion? Not sure what you're interested in? Get out of your comfort zone and challenge yourself by trying something new! If you consider watching movies, social media spiraling, or playing video games hobbies then technically you're not wrong. But for the purposes of career exploration, I would like you to focus on exploring productive hobbies. Productive hobbies, or pro-hobbies as I call them, are activities that you enjoy doing in your spare time which develops a skill or explores a profession. A few good examples of pro-hobbies are photography, creative writing, launching a YouTube channel, learning how to photoshop, playing an instrument, etc. Trying a pro-hobby may not directly lead to a pursuit of a career pathway, but you will learn something about yourself in the process and maybe even develop a valuable new skill if you really give it your best effort.

Walt Disney once said, "We keep moving forward, opening new

doors, and doing new things, because we're curious and curiosity keeps leading us down new paths."[30] There are hidden pathways that won't be visible until you start to move forward. I tried rapping and producing, which led me to writing spoken word poetry and authorship. It's time for you to move and try something new. Get creative and think of different pro-hobbies that may interest you. If you need some inspiration you can find an expansive list of hobbies on the website www.hobbyhelp.com.

What pro-hobby would you like to try?

Extracurricular/Recreational Activities

> *Extracurricular activity – An activity, performed by students, that falls outside the realm of the normal curriculum of school, college or university education.*[31]
>
> *Recreational activity – Something a person does for fun and enjoyment.*[32]

I always loved playing basketball. I remember spending countless hours at the basketball court with my older brother, just two kids with dreams of mastering Allen Iverson's crossover and the spectacular antics of Rafer Alston (aka Skip to My Lou). After beating my brother for years on end, I wanted to test my game and see how good I really was. I decided to try out for the basketball team as a freshman in high school. That was the moment that I realized the organized game was more sophisticated than the streetball game I grew up with. For the first time I went up against kids who had been playing organized basketball for years and knew where to be, when to pass, when to shoot, and how to play zone defense. When I didn't make the cut, I understood that there were levels to this game. Failing to make the team didn't cause me to love playing basketball any less. However, I soon realized that at my then height of 5'6" and weight of 150 pounds, I didn't have the physical giftings to make it to the NBA. Because I loved playing the game, I felt that making the junior varsity team was still in reach if I committed to working on my game. Over the next year, I invested more time working on my game, and sure enough, I made the team! And I set the basketball world on fire! On the season, I scored two points, made zero baskets, and played about eight minutes total of game action! Realizing the world would never embrace a player as dominant as myself, in the spirit of fair competition, I decided that I would leave the professional sports pathway behind.

My storied high school basketball career may not have ended in MVPs, state championships, or even a related career path, but it did cause me to learn more about an interest that I enjoy watching and playing even today. I learned the value of being on a team, how to take directions, that competition is a motivating force, that investing my time and energy will lead to improvement, that how you play the game is as important as winning itself, and that practice and repetition builds self-confidence. All those lessons I learned back then are even more applicable to my life off the court today.

If you're currently in school, then consider going beyond your academic studies and participating in things that will supplement your educational experience. It can be basketball, a debate team, art club, yearbook club, a cultural club, a chess team, etc. Just try *something*! You'll be amazed at the things you learn and the new relationships that can be formed around a common interest. Most schools have a listing of the different activities that are offered and may have an event in which students can sign up for different clubs. Ask around and see what's out there! If you are out of school, consider participating in recreational activities that may be offered by your employer or in the local community.

Which extracurricular and/or recreational activities offered would you like to explore?

Job Shadowing/Internship/Part-time Work (Students)

Internship – The position of a student or trainee who works in an organization, sometimes without pay, in order to gain work experience or satisfy requirements for a qualification.[33]

Job Shadowing – An activity where one can observe, and follow someone in your potential field while the professional is at work.[34]

Part-time work – Paid on-the-job work experience for a duration that is less than a full-time schedule.

My first internship experience was not what I expected. As a rising senior at Lincoln High School, I found a paid internship at a plumbing supply company that was a short ten-minute bike ride away from my home. The expectation was that I would work in the office and learn the accounting and bookkeeping part of the business, but I spent the entire summer gathering plumbing supply orders, loading and unloading trucks, sweeping a dusty warehouse, and learning all sorts of new swear words from a couple of the wise warehouse veterans. It wasn't what I expected, but I learned a lot about the type of career that I didn't want for myself. I was certain that laboring in the sweltering heat of summer or in the frigid frost of winter would not be my thing.

I summoned the courage to communicate to the general manager my expectation to learn about the accounting and bookkeeping side of the business. Because I gave my best effort and demonstrated professionalism in the warehouse labor role, he offered me a part-time role in their office on the second floor. It wasn't much more glamorous than the warehouse role, but it did provide the comforts of air conditioning in the summer and heat in the winter. I had to learn how to answer phones, organize paperwork, file invoices, and dust and vacuum the office before I learned even a little bit about accounting. My part-time work at the plumbing supply place ended the summer before I went to Pace University. That very summer, I had another internship opportunity at Pepsi

Bottling Group where I actually learned about the accounting side of the business.

I don't know why I imagined accounting would be more engaging, but I quickly grew tired of the repetitive tasks and the mundane nature of the job. The upside was that the pay for the accounting work was much higher than the manual labor, so I figured I would continue on that route and see where the money led me. If you read the previous chapters, you know exactly where the money led . . . it led me to write this book about the importance of living inspired.

Time after time, I've found that my expectations of a job, internship, or career have differed from reality. Job shadowing, internships, and part-time work offer you the opportunity to preview a potential career path and determine whether a pathway piques your interest or is just not for you. Whether your experience is enjoyable or unsatisfying, previewing a potential career path will teach you new skills and provide useful information about what engages you. In your preview, you are not looking for the perfect career path where you are excited about every aspect of the job. That's not realistic. What you're looking for within the preview opportunity is the elements of it that engage you and connect to your noble goal, your larger sense of purpose. Once you identify those elements, you can decide whether the pathway is worth further exploration. Maybe there is no perfect career path that is completely devoid of meaningless and trivial tasks. However:

There is a career path that will allow you to optimize your skills and talents, spend more time in your passion, and connect to your sense of purpose. Nothing will bring you closer to finding that than living the pathway. Nothing confirms like experience.

Time to live inspired! Your high school or college may have a job shadowing program, internship program, or part-time work listing available to you. Investigate what resources may be available through your school and identify the opportunities that may be of interest to you. You can also search for part-time work and internship opportunities on popular national websites like:

www.handshake.com – For college students seeking jobs and internships.
www.internships.com – For high school, undergraduate, and graduate students seeking jobs and internships.
www.linkedin.com – For students and professionals seeking job and career opportunities.
www.indeed.com – For students and professionals seeking job and career opportunities.

Are there job shadowing, internship, or part-time work programs/listings offered by your school? If so, which opportunities would you like to explore?

Which job shadowing, internship, or part-time work opportunities listed on one of the popular websites would you like to explore?

Mentorship

> *Mentorship – A relationship between two people where the individual with more experience, knowledge, and connections is able to pass along what they have learned to a more junior individual within a certain field. The more senior individual is the mentor, and the more junior individual is the mentee.*[35]

There's wisdom in following in the footsteps of someone who has accomplished something similar to what you would like to accomplish. Identifying a mentor who can guide you on your path to success can help you avoid traps and mistakes along your chosen path. You can find a mentor in your own home, your extended family, your place of worship, your school, or at work.

The Ideal Mentor:

- Has a direct or indirect personal connection to you.
- Is succeeding in a path that you would like to follow.
- Has unique knowledge, experience, wisdom and discernment.
- Is a positive person and positive example morally and ethically
- Is willing to make themselves available to you

The ideal mentor has a direct or indirect (i.e., friend of a relative) connection with you and is therefore more invested in your growth and development. The ideal mentor has achieved some success in a path like the one you would like to follow. It is a given that a mentor should have unique knowledge, experience, and wisdom to share that is applicable to you and your journey. But an overlooked attribute of an ideal mentor is discernment in sharing the right advice, at the right time, in the right tone and context so that their contribution to your growth can be most effective. The ideal mentor needs to have the wherewithal to deliver negative feedback in a way that is still encouraging to the mentee. It isn't required that the ideal mentor is always positive and protects you from constructive criticism, but it is important that your mentor is a positive example morally and ethically.

Of course, none of these attributes matter if your mentor is unwilling or unable to share their time with you. It's important that you have a connection with the ideal mentor, as they will likely be more willing to make themselves available to you on a consistent basis. Keep in mind that those who are committed to success are weary of distractions that can pull them away from achieving their own goals. Ideally, your mentor needs to be someone who can make themselves available to you at a minimum for at least fifteen to thirty minutes once or twice every three months if needed.

In establishing a mentorship, it's up to you as the mentee to initiate and try to make it a formal relationship. Ask directly, "I respect the work that you're doing and I aspire to do something similar. If you have the time available, would you consider meeting with me for about twenty minutes each month to discuss my personal, academic, and professional growth? I understand that your schedule may be quite busy, so I'm open to an occasional informal conversation from time to time as well." This approach communicates your expectations as a mentee, gives the other party a chance to set the parameters of the relationship, and provides the other party an opportunity to politely decline due to time constraints. If the person you ask declines a formal relationship, don't take it personally. It may not be the best time for them to take on additional obligations. And if they say no, then trust me, they're doing you a favor. Their honesty is preventing the unfortunate situation where a mentee feels neglected by a mentor that is unresponsive to communication. This can cause feelings of discontentment that may harm a current relationship that may have been beneficial in the future.

Having an effective mentor can help you navigate the twists and turns within a career path. But a mentor is just one person who is on TEAM YOU! Your mentor's role is to support you as you pursue your SMART goals by providing guidance, wisdom, and encouragement along the way. Think critically about who the ideal mentor for you may be and choose wisely! It's up to you to initiate and formalize the mentor relationship. And it's up to you to make great use of their time for your own benefit. If you would like more information on establishing and maintaining an effective mentorship relationship, consider reading *Mentorship: The Playbook* by author, speaker, and financial professional Rahkim Sabree.

Considering the career pathway(s) that interest you, who might be your ideal mentor(s)?

Building a support system is critical to your success. A support system can lift you up when you get down and help you remain committed to achieving your goal. The next chapter asks the question, "Are you willing to commit to achieve your goal?" I hope your immediate response is an emphatic "YES!" But what does it mean to be committed? And how do you maintain your commitment when the going gets tough? I have a few tips to share. But first, let's practice EQ.

Practice EQ

1. **Pursue Noble Goals – Key Takeaway #3**
   a. Develop a SMART goal based on pursuing a particular career pathway and describe how it is connected to your noble goal.
   b. Develop two to three SMART goals based on actions you can take today to begin exploring a hobby, extracurricular activity, volunteer opportunity or other career preview opportunity. If you have already identified one of your talents, consider participating in an activity that will strengthen and enhance it. If you've identified a passion of yours, consider participating in a cause or activity that will allow you to sustain that energy and share it with others. Group activities are preferred over individual ones. To accelerate your growth, place yourself around others who will encourage your exploration, challenge you, and nurture your talents.
2. Recognize Patterns – BUILD Emotional Intelligence
   a. Specifically describe a time when you felt overwhelmed, stressed, frustrated, or angered during an academic, extracurricular, recreational, or work-related activity.
      i. Reflection:
         1. What emotion did you feel and what was your outward response? Did you quit, make sarcastic comments, put others down, use sarcasm, stay quiet, cross your arms in protest, choose to ignore what has happening, silently protest, ask questions to further understand, change your perspective, ask for help, etc.?
         2. Think about other times when you have felt the same emotion. Do you recognize a pattern in your outward response to the emotion?

3. Revisiting the situation you described, how would you use the BUILD model to navigate your emotions and choose the best response for the situation.

3. Apply Consequential Thinking – Team Me
   a. You've already started to build Team Me when you identified a supportive classmate, coworker, friend, or relative who you feel comfortable sharing your progress toward achieving your goals. But every good team needs an experienced coaching staff to help guide them to a championship. Take another step toward building your championship team by using the ideal mentor criteria to identify and select one or two individuals to be your mentor. As part of your coaching staff, your mentor's role is to help you think through strategies and best practices to further your development and help you achieve your goals. Your mentor is not thinking FOR you, they are thinking WITH you. As you strategize and plan with them, bring a perspective or point of view, so they can opine, provide insight, and effectively advise. So who will be the Phil Jackson to your Michael Jordan? Why is the person an ideal mentor for you? How and when will you try to formalize the mentor/mentee relationship?

Notes

Notes

FOUR

Are you willing to commit to achieving your goals?

Crossroad

What do you do when you're at a crossroad and neither road leads to home?
You shutter in fear, stand there and make a decision alone
You pray one road leads to a throne, a crown, an audience, a bow
But what if both roads are despair, a drop, a door that's locked, a hate pot pie, a mistake, a lie…
You stand and ponder, wait a bit longer
Pray for direction, you stay
Correction…
You freeze in panic, your heartbeat is static
It slows, it thumps, you stumble, you front
You pretend to be plotting, you're scared,
You're stopping, you're pensive…

This road isn't for you, that's the truth
Concocted, created, convinced, believed
A lie turned fact, a choice, a pact, YOUR DECISION
So you settle. You have peace. It lasts for a week.
Then you're weak and you're pale, can't sleep, and you sneeze

And you cough, you're diseased, you're blind
You can't see that you've lost what you need to cross and it stings!
This is a life threatening infection
You will either thrive or die
The cure is effort, but the fear of failure is paralyzing
So you lie there in the dark, waiting for the end
But it's a slow death
The loud tick of the clock becomes too much to bear

You CHOOSE resistance, you heighten your senses
Feel your way through the dark, you get up and march.
Momentum builds, you hobble, then step, you SCREAM
you fall, you bleed, you sweat, you cry
You inhale what you thought was your very last breath
Yet…you step…step…step…

What is the major theme of the Crossroad poem? How does the theme apply to you?

Commitment – The act of binding yourself (intellectually or emotionally) to a course of action.[36]

"Crossroad" is one of my favorite poems. I know that parts of it are a little dark, but there's a powerful light at the end of the tunnel! I wrote this poem around the time that I created my company KS4Inspiration. At that time, I was just beginning to truly believe that I could achieve my goal of positively impacting my community through the arts. It was the second or third poem I had written after a long hiatus. My performance skills were rusty, and I expected that it would be a challenge to build a following from scratch. I knew many obstacles existed on the path I chose to walk and I understood that it would be difficult to make the impact I felt I was spiritually called to make. Yet, I persisted because I found myself energized by the creative process and emboldened by my ability to problem solve. Even when a poem didn't quite hit the audience as hard as I hoped, I kept going. Even when a school told me they didn't have room in their budget for a program, I executed it anyhow. And when my performance opportunities slowed down and the poems became harder to craft with high quality, it was only my commitment mindset that pushed me to continue. Unlike the earlier years, when I gave up on my musical aspirations in order to pursue my professional goals, this time around I have a committed mindset and am focused on using my poetic powers for good. I am my best hype man, positively reinforcing my commitment with my words "Kev, you got this!" "This poem is fire," "Go head and swag on them." I am demonstrating my commitment with the moves that I make by creating www.KS4Inspiration.com, sharing inspirational images on @KS4Inspiration, and sharing game with the youth in our high schools and colleges whenever I can. With each move that I make, my momentum builds, making the next step on my journey a little bit easier.

You can be committed in your thoughts, you can express commitment in your words, but you can only demonstrate commitment in your actions. Said another way, commitment begins with your mind, is reinforced in your messaging, and is realized in the moves that you make.

This is what I call the three M's of commitment: Mind, Message, Moves. The proof of commitment is the last M, Move, which represents the micro and macro steps you take toward achieving your goal.

This chapter asks the question, "Are you willing to commit to achieving your goals?" I presume most will quickly respond, "Yes, I am!" That's great! It really is! But I have a few follow-up questions. What is the proof of your commitment? How do you respond when the going gets tough? When your progress has stalled? When your plan is interrupted? When factors out of your control indicate that you need to change course? It's easy to remain committed to a goal when things are easy and the path is clear. But the true test of commitment arises when you face a challenge and the outcome is uncertain. In this chapter, you will analyze how you can remain committed to your goals despite the obstacles that will come. Through the lens of KS4Inspiration's three M's of commitment, you will focus your mind, refine your messaging, and make strategic moves to remain committed to achieving your goals.

Focus Your Mind

Remember the noble goal and SMART goals you developed a while back? A noble goal is a brief and compelling statement of purpose that helps you evaluate your choices (ex. To inspire others to live purposefully). Your SMART goals are destinations you aspire to reach as you live within your noble goal (ex. Work full-time as a mechanical engineer at Disney World after graduating from college). As you walk the road of success toward each SMART goal, you will meet many obstacles. You will have tough days that cause you to question whether you can really achieve your goal or whether the goal is even worth the effort.

This is where your noble goal comes into play. Your noble goal is your "why." It plays a big role in maintaining commitment to your goals. When you crush your interview for your dream job but don't get an offer, or you apply for a competitive science program at an Ivy League university and are waitlisted, it's important that you remember your why. Why is it important for me to achieve that goal? Maybe you aspire to develop new medical technology that will prevent another global pandemic. Maybe you were seeking the respect of friends or your parents. If your SMART goal is truly aligned with your noble goal and you are intrinsically motivated to see it through, then bounce back like Big Sean and try again, or find an alternative pathway that leads to the same or a similar impact.

Commitment is not about trying to break through a cement wall with your bare fist. It is about evaluating your options to overcome obstacles in order to achieve the ultimate goal.

So if your SMART goal is truly aligned with your noble goal, and worth your time and effort, focus your mind on your why and find a way through. Don't give up! When you struggle at that first wall it's easy to become overwhelmed by thinking of the many more walls that await ahead. Don't be discouraged! Remember that the journey is one step at a time.

Focus your mind on today's solutions for today's obstacles. When your road of success isn't meeting expectations, you're feeling overwhelmed, or you face rejection and failure, don't strike at the cement wall due to pride, frustration, and stubbornness. Save your knuckles! Survey your surroundings, and find the right door to walk through, the sturdiest rope to climb over, or a strong shovel to tunnel under. It is easier to do this if you focus your mind on your why, reminding yourself of the important reason that you continue on.

How does your noble goal help you maintain your commitment?

To Focus Your Mind:

- Remember your why! Reflecting on your noble goal reengages your intrinsic motivation.
- Focus on what you can do today. Don't overwhelm yourself trying to solve tomorrow's problems.
- Identify alternative solutions that allow you to continue your journey.

Refine Your Messages

There will be days when you doubt that you can, or, like in the poem "Crossroad," you decide that you won't. How do you refine your message and get back on track? In and of itself, feeling motivated will not be enough. Motivation has an expiration date. Like any other emotion, the feeling of being motivated intensifies and fades. Commitment speaks to your willingness to continue your journey even when your motivation is low. On those days when the fear of failure is overwhelming, or you "just don't feel like it," will you bury your head in the sand to distract yourself, or will you keep your head up and march forward? It's up to you to formulate a plan of action to address the periods of low motivation that threaten your ability to achieve your goals.

How will you energize yourself when your mind is consumed with thoughts of falling short of your goals? As I expressed in the "Crossroad" poem, the fear of failure is paralyzing. The emotion of fear is thought of as a negative emotion, but it is essential to our safety. When humankind were only cave dwellers who needed to duck and dodge dangerous predators, it was the feeling of fear that prompted us to survive by sheltering in place and waiting until the threat had passed. In the present day, we use the fear mechanism to help us avoid cars as we cross the street and take a different route home after school to avoid Nicky's crew. The emotion of fear is also being repurposed for dinner parties, first dates, public speaking, SAT exams, job interviews, and many other crucial goals.

I need you to recognize that when you feel fearful as you approach the next crucial step toward your goals, it is not a signal to shelter in place or run in

the opposite direction. Instead, it is an opportunity to be courageous.

To flip that fear into courage, you must convince yourself of your ability to persevere by reflecting on all the obstacles you've already overcome to reach this pivotal moment. If you're reading this, you are old enough to have experienced some degree of suffering and struggle in your life. You have persevered over your academic struggles, sexual or physical abuse, the foster care system, depression, anxiety, drug addiction, bullying, gang violence, self-esteem issues, identity crisis, poverty, bad break ups, learning disabilities, eating disorders, and the like! You have persevered and you have not quit! You have already proven that you can be courageous when facing your fear. So take the next step in your journey with confidence, knowing that no matter the outcome, you have faced your fears with courage, providing further evidence of your resiliency.

How will you respond on those lazy days when you're feeling discouraged and would rather do anything in the world besides putting in work? In situations like this, you will need to refine your messaging in order to boost your morale. Verbalize to yourself, "I'm committed to the work," "I can do this," "Nothing will stop me!" You have to be your own hype man! I encouraged you to build TEAM ME to help support and encourage you, but YOU are without a doubt your biggest supporter! If you can master the art of refining your messaging, you will be able to provide the gas to get your engine running. So shout those positive affirmations at a mirror, leave positive notes on your refrigerator, change your cell phone background to your favorite bible verse, hang that motivational poster on your wall, create a playlist of your favorite inspirational songs. Do whatever you need to do to offset the impact of discouraging thoughts and emotions.

When you don't have the strength or discipline to stay with it, remember that you have TEAM ME there to encourage and guide you as well. A mentor or educator can provide a different perspective on how to solve a problem, your friends can show you how they overcame a similar obstacle, your parents and siblings can hopefully provide emotional support. Studies have shown that we can increase the odds of achieving our goals by writing them down and sharing our progress with an encouraging person. Having someone you trust hold you accountable for your action and inaction is a proven useful tool, so look to your team to help hold you accountable when you're contemplating a "temporary" pause in your journey.

When your internal messages don't provide the gas for your engine, look to your team for the steam to power through.

To Refine Your Messages:

- Reflect on your progress! It is encouraging evidence of your ability to overcome obstacles.
- Be your own hype man! Remind yourself regularly that you can and you will.
- Lean on your team! For encouragement and accountability.

What action(s) will you take to refine your messaging when feeling discouraged or fearful on the road of success?

Make Strategic Moves

Years ago, I decided to change the trajectory of my career by becoming a certified financial planner. In order to do it, I needed to prepare a financial planning case study, complete a review course, and study about fifteen to twenty hours per week for about one year, in order to then pass a six-hour exam. I decided that the best time to do this would be when I had plenty of time, no excuses, and zero distractions. I obviously chose to do this only mere months after officially moving my family from Queens to Yonkers, the birth of my second son, and beginning a new career pathway on a new team in a new city. My timing couldn't be more perfect! There were many days early on when I felt broke, busted, and disgusted. I knew that I needed to put in more time studying to pass the exam, but I had every excuse not to study. Our newborn was crying in the middle of the night and every morning I went into work tired and came home even more exhausted. I needed time to just Netflix and chillax, before spending time with my family, and doing it all over again the next day. I was inconsistent with my studying to say the least, but because I remained committed to the goal I didn't give in to my legitimate excuses. Instead, I used my problem-solving skills to overcome my excuses, limit my distractions, and make consistent moves.

"I know I need to study, but I'm just too exhausted to do it after working a full day and tending to my family." This was my standard excuse for the Monday to Friday workday grind. It felt like a legitimate excuse because the fatigue was real, and spending time with family is a priority for me. But I found a way around this by adjusting my schedule. Psychology research shows that the most productive time to work is the first two hours after you wake up, when your mind is fresh and decision fatigue has yet to set in.[37] On most workdays, I decided to set my wake up alarm for four a.m., a few hours earlier than normal, in order to get my study hours in before my workday began. In order to wake up at four, I needed to get to bed by ten p.m., a couple hours earlier than normal. I usually arrived home each night by seven, which meant that I had three hours to split between eating dinner, spending time with my wife and kids, relaxing, and indulging in distractions.

What excuse(s) have you used for releasing yourself of a commitment to a goal?

Something had to give, and I knew what that something was. Prior to rearranging my schedule, my wife and I would spend our evenings getting lost in an endless social media loop or watching our favorite tv shows until about midnight. These were the distractions that I needed to drastically limit. With regard to social media, Facebook and Instagram are enough for me. I'll leave Snapchat, TikTok, Patreon and whatever else follows to generation Z. Y'all don't want me there, and I don't want to be there! While I found it easy to limit my social media usage, I have to admit that Netflix was and is a more formidable foe. I've been trying to slay that dragon for years now, yet it persists. Because Netflix is a useful form of distraction and relaxation for me, I've decided to control the time and place of our interaction. I schedule time to chill just like I schedule time to grind, making sure my time is appropriately allocated in order to avoid burnout and move intentionally toward my goals.

Left unchecked, distractions will keep you from taking steps toward your goals (watching Netflix *instead* of writing your book) or from taking *effective* steps toward your goals (watching Netflix *while* "writing" your book). Distractions need to be identified and either eliminated or limited. Eliminate the obviously unhealthy distractions such as drugs and comparing yourself to others. Limit the other distractions that can become unhealthy in excess, such as video games, television, and social media. The people in our lives can distract or deter us as well, but that's a longer story for a different chapter. For now, just remember to surround yourself with individuals that are driven, encouraging, and possess integrity while building Team ME.

Once you have your distractions under control, you must rededicate that time to consistent productive action. The key word here is consistency! When you make consistent moves, you develop habits that will propel you toward your goals. The word habit is defined as an acquired mode of behavior that has become nearly or completely involuntary.[38] How amazing would it be to have your natural instincts pull you toward your desired outcome? According to a 2009 study, on average it takes about sixty-six days for a new habit to stick.[39] If you can make consistent moves for a little longer than two months, you will be more likely to stick with it thereafter. Taking consistent action helps you build momentum that will make the process a little less strenuous as you move forward. Your momentum will prevent you from becoming complacent, second guessing your efforts, and taking that temporary break that eventually becomes indefinite.

Take my story for example. It wasn't easy at first, but day after day I stuck to the plan of getting to bed early and waking early. Eventually, my body adjusted and I was naturally exhausted by nine p.m. and I was waking up minutes before my alarm went off at four. My mind was fresh and I was able to study longer and more effectively. Each study session built confidence in my ability to achieve my goal. I was encouraged each time I was able to apply what I learned at work, motivating me to study more. It was a powerful motivational loop that built momentum, making the walk toward my goals just a little bit easier.

Obstacles come in many forms including excuses and distractions. If you can take consistent actions to overcome your obstacles, you can develop helpful habits that will make the bumpy ride to the top of the mountain just a little bit smoother. In my case, I needed to make strategic moves to maintain my commitment to passing a CFP exam. You may need to make strategic moves to increase your GPA, earn a promotion at work, learn to play the piano, make the soccer team, start a new business, write a book, or develop a new software app. Whatever your goal may be, you will need to overcome your excuses, control your distractions, and take consistent action to build momentum that propels you toward your goals.

Make Strategic Moves That:

- Eliminate excuses! Everyone's got one…what will you do about yours?
- Get out of your own way! Reduce or eliminate distractions that keep you from taking steps toward your goals.
- Develop new habits! Consistency builds momentum that propels you toward your goals.

Is something keeping you from taking more substantial steps toward your goals? What strategic moves might you implement to maintain your commitment?

How much free time do you have during the weekend? Weekdays? How could you best use that time to achieve your goals?

Emotional Decision-Making

You ever found yourself in an emotional state where you lost control and made an impulsive decision? We've all been there at one time or another. Whether you were frustrated during basketball practice and decided to walk out, or you were disappointed by a friend and stopped following them on IG, everyone has had a moment when their emotions were the driver and they were just a passenger along for the ride. In the Six Seconds world we call this hijacking, referring to the term amygdala hijacking first made popular by emotional intelligence expert Daniel Goleman. To simplify the brain science behind hijacking, in cases where we perceive a threat, our thalamus skips the thinking and processing cortex and reroutes our impulse directly to the amygdala where peptides and hormones create emotion and action, tapping into previously stored patterns of reaction in order to quickly respond to the threat. The hijacked state, when your brain is flooded with these electro-chemicals, only lasts three to six seconds.[40] So if you can pause long enough for your cortical brain to catch up, you will allow the intensity of the emotion to pass so that you can then form a more thoughtful response!

Why is it important to pause when at a highly emotional crossroad?

We are at a crossroad with each decision we make. In the moment, it's not always clear whether the decision to be made is critical or nominal. Your emotions during the decision-making process may influence your judgment positively or negatively. When at a crossroad, if you pause to think about what you're feeling and why, you can allow the intensity of the emotion to subside and then thoughtfully consider the best course of action.

Pausing provides you the space to use your emotions as one source of information (not the only source) to help you avoid an impulsive emotional response and make a thoughtful decision that is in line with the outcome you truly desire.

Developing the skill of managing our emotions will help us remain committed to our goals even when we arrive at the highly emotional crossroads of our lives. Each time you arrive at a key juncture, remember to pause, allow the intensity of the moment to pass, and then form a thoughtful response allowing you to proceed on the road of success with confidence. After all, in order to achieve, you must believe! You'll explore what you believe about yourself in the next chapter. But first, let's practice EQ!

Practice EQ

1. **Exercise Optimism – Key Takeaway #4**
    a. Reflect on one or two of the SMART goals you previously set. When approaching obstacles that threaten your commitment, what actions can you take to:
        i. Focus your mind to remind you of your why and engage intrinsic motivation?
            1. *Ex. Brainstorm with a parent, mentor, or guidance counselor on different strategies or pathways to overcome obstacles.*
            2. *Ex. Make a daily to-do list in order to be present and focus on overcoming today's obstacles.*
        ii. Refine your messaging to exercise optimism?
            1. *Ex. Create a playlist of inspirational and motivational songs.*
            2. *Ex. Practice mindfulness or pray daily finding strength in your faith.*
        iii. Make strategic moves to promote consistency?
            1. *Ex. Share my progress toward my goal with a friend weekly.*
            2. *Ex. Limit television/social media usage to an hour per day on the weekdays.*
2. Recognizing Patterns
    a. Describe a time when you made an important decision or responded to someone while in a highly emotional state.
        i. Looking back, are you satisfied with the outcome of your response?

   ii. How would you respond differently in a similar situation in the future?

b. Time inventory – How much free time do you have each day? How will you use that time to take steps toward your goals and exploring your interests?

Notes

Notes

Notes

FIVE

Do you believe that you can achieve your goals?

Accept Yourself

I am cut from a different cloth
A square on a quilt
Never quite fit in with a squad or a clique
Hated on for a difference in the way that I think
Saw no value in a chain or pink chinchilla mink
I had ambition before I knew that it was fuel for a mission
Headed somewhere fast, the destination was missing

I raised my hand in class to ask and answer the question
They would laugh and smirk, like "Ha! Dude is a nerd!"
Yeah I heard, yeah it hurt, yeah it's words, yeah i cared,
Yeah I splurged on some Avirex, Tims, Girbauds
Got fresh to get them off my neck, next step was get the girls
Now I'm cool cause I'm "ghetto" but I couldn't drop the nerd…

I guess fitting in wasn't meant to be
When I think about it, even my tormentors saw something
different in me

It took me long enough, but now I finally see
I was gifted with a drive for the mission
Uniquely designed for a path less traveled
So I smash your gavel if you judge my craft

Foolishness says to be one in a crowd
But the smart money, is to be one in a thou
You are gifted! Don't be afraid to announce it
With all the naysayers in the world trying to denounce it
You are more than enough, just accept yourself
And realize nothing is in your way...except yourself
When you hit the roadblock, accept some help
When you climb that mountain, lift someone else
That's the greatest law, right? To love thy neighbor?
Even if that neighbor...is a hater

My poem "Accept Yourself" highlights my longing for acceptance from others during my teenage and early adult years. I remember feeling like I didn't quite fit in with different cliques. In high school, I didn't love the tough guy, dog-eat-dog atmosphere of the basketball team. I knew I had to emit that type of energy just so I could survive the experience, but that wasn't really me. I knew it and my teammates knew it. Kendrick said, "You don't have to lie to kick it…" and he ain't never lied! Eventually I found a group of classmates that accepted me for who I was. My self-esteem increased as I formed new and healthy friendships. I valued being my authentic self and felt compelled to save room for others to be themselves as well. I was and am playful, friendly, encouraging, swag-tastic, competitive, focused, and respectful. Eventually, I came to understand that my contribution to the world would be sourced from the uniqueness of my character and life experiences. On the road of success, you too will struggle to identify how you fit in to different environments. There are times that you may feel unworthy, rejected, and out of place amongst coworkers, classmates, teammates, family, and friends. Instead of desperately seeking the approval of others, find peace in accepting your true self, knowing that you have value just as you are.

> To be anything other than your authentic self is to rob the world of the gifts that you were uniquely made to offer.

Do you truly accept yourself? What would it feel like to be your most authentic self among family, friends, and peers?

Deconstructive Harmful Feedback

Deconstructive harmful feedback – A criticism or comment that is false, unactionable, or intentionally hurtful.

Self-esteem – Self-esteem refers to the positive (high self-esteem) or negative (low self-esteem) feelings that we have about ourselves.[41]

How you feel about yourself, whether positive (high) or negative (low), is the result of what you do and the type of relationships that you form with others. Acing a test, learning a new skill, being recognized as employee of the month, and receiving likes and comments on your social media posts generally build your esteem. Likewise, missing the honor roll, not making the softball team, being passed over for promotion, or experiencing the end of a close relationship can lower your self-esteem. It's difficult to believe that you can achieve your goals when you don't believe in yourself, when you don't believe in your ability to learn and grow. In the previous chapter I encouraged you to focus your mind, refine your messaging, and make strategic moves to remain committed to achieving your goals. That same advice is applicable to building and maintaining a positive self-esteem.

If you can maintain a positive self-esteem, you can defend yourself against deconstructive feedback that may demoralize and paralyze you. In the previous chapter, I mentioned that some people around you may be an obstacle in your road of success. Many of us don't realize the powerful effect that others have on our self-esteem. In our conversations, text messages, social media posts and views, we're constantly receiving feedback on who we are and how we're perceived. Twenty-four seven social feedback is a relatively new phenomenon. Back in the day, the social feedback from our peers would end at the end of the school or workday. Now the feedback continues online and is stored in archives that we can revisit again and again. If all the feedback were positive, that would be a great thing! Except, we know for a fact that's not the case. We feel the sting of harsh judgment, unfair criticism, and vicious "jokes" daily. It comes from fellow students, coworkers, "close" friends, teammates, educators, siblings, and parents. Many go through the day without a single positive comment, a high-five, or a pat on the back. And sometimes home isn't a safe haven from a harsh and critical world.

This is not constructive negative feedback which can help build you up. This is deconstructive harmful feedback that is meant to break you down. I need you to identify this type of harmful feedback and reject it on its face! DJ Khaled famously states that "they don't want you to win." "They" is anyone intentionally discouraging you from taking action. "They" are those that amplify your shortcomings and overlook your strengths. "They" identify the problems and couldn't care less about the solution. "They" say you can't because your parents didn't. "They" say you won't so that you begin to believe it. "They" are not invested in your success because it reminds them of their failures. "They" are hurt and want to share their pain. "They" are enemies. "They" are strangers. "They" are "friends." "They" are family. "They" is systemic racism, misogyny, homophobia, and xenophobia.

"They" will erect physical, societal, and legislative walls to block you. The walls will be so formidable and intimidating that some won't dare attempt to supersede them. But *you* will. Because "they" are not all powerful, "they" can be overcome. Your walk on the road of success will be the proof.

So I urge you to accept yourself! Focus your mind, refine your messages, and make strategic moves that will build your self-esteem so that you will believe in yourself and effectively block malicious attacks on your road of success. This may mean some relationships need to change or end. You may need to form or strengthen relationships with positive and encouraging individuals. You may have to refine your messaging and affirm that you are worthy of love, support, and success. You may have to focus your mind on your "why" so you can recognize that social media commentary is not important or relevant to your mission. Bottomline is you need a strategy to protect your sense of self from those who want to see you fall.

How will you protect your self-esteem from deconstructive harmful feedback?

Constructive Negative Feedback

Constructive negative feedback – Actionable and thoughtful criticism that communicates areas for growth and improvement.

Self-compassion – A willingness to look at your own mistakes and shortcomings with kindness and understanding.[42]

Growth mindset – A belief that one's intelligence and most basic abilities can be developed.

Fixed mindset – A belief that one's intelligence and most basic abilities are relatively set and determined.

While I maintain that having a positive self-esteem is a helpful defense against deconstructive harmful feedback, a 2012 study authored by Juliana Breines and Serena Chen found that those who exercised self-compassion were more likely to see their weaknesses as changeable. Self-compassion actually increased their motivation to improve and avoid the same mistake again in the future.[43] Kristin Neff, a professor at the University of Texas and researcher in the field of self-compassion, has explained that "self-compassion entails being warm and understanding towards oneself when encountering suffering, inadequacy or failure, rather than ignoring one's pain or flagellating oneself with self-criticism."[44]

For example, if an employer didn't offer you the job after a sub-par interview, you would naturally feel disappointed. But rather than conclude that you're a poor interviewee, you would exercise self-compassion by acknowledging that you can learn from the mistakes you made during the interview. Instead of wallowing in self-pity, you will prepare for your next interview opportunity and practice communicating your work experience and career goals in a clear and concise manner.

Exercising self-compassion triggers people to adopt what Stanford psychologist Carol Dweck calls a *growth mindset.* If you believe that your characteristics, aptitudes, and abilities can be changed, then you can embrace challenges, view effort as essential to your development, accept constructive negative feedback, and learn from others. Because you acknowledge your potential for growth, you are more likely to feel motivated to put in the work and move forward. However, if you have a *fixed mindset*, you believe that your characteristics, aptitudes, and abilities are set in stone—therefore you lack the incentive to pursue further growth.[45] In order to truly believe that you can achieve your goals, a growth mindset is required.

When you begin your journey on day one, you may not possess the skills and experience needed to achieve your ultimate goal, but you must possess the mindset that will allow you to grow into the version of you that will one day get there.

Self-compassion is particularly important when it comes to effectively addressing negative feedback. When I say negative feedback, I don't mean people hating on you. I mean constructive negative feedback from individuals that are invested in your development, like a trusted educator, coach, mentor, wise friend, sibling, or parent. For example, a mentor at work who calls you out for lacking the initiative to help your team, a parent who cautions you to be mindful of your tone of voice when speaking to others (and especially them), a coach who encourages you to practice your free throws if you want to see more time on the court, or a guidance counselor who urges you to put more effort into studying AP history in order to get into your dream school.

As you travel the road of success, you will need to actively seek opportunities for personal development. I asked you to build TEAM ME so that you could have access to trusted individuals who can hold you accountable to your goals and be a source of valuable constructive feedback that can accelerate your development. Sometimes negative feedback from strangers can be helpful. Because they don't know you, they may be more willing to give you the honest, unfiltered truth. On the other hand, if you have the same feedback delivered by an individual you trust, the feedback may still sting, but you may be more likely to accept and address it. Not everyone on TEAM ME may be willing to give you negative feedback. Your ace is more likely to boost you up than to say anything that may hurt you, and that's ok! They are playing the supportive friend role that they're comfortable with. It's up to you to use your discretion in determining where to go for the real (Hint: NOT SOCIAL MEDIA!). So identify a few reliable sources of truth and request constructive feedback regularly.

Speaking from experience, it's impossible to receive negative feedback independent of emotions. Each piece of feedback you receive is immediately processed in the mind as either true or false, or good or bad, and a corresponding emotion will follow—discouraged, disappointed, frustrated, apathetic, etc. You've learned enough about emotional intelligence by now to know that it's ok to feel these emotions, but you don't want to let the intensity of the emotions dictate your response. Instead, you will exercise self-compassion to effectively navigate your emotions and choose a growth-minded response. Easier said than done, I know! No worries, I have a few tips that, with practice over time, will help you effectively respond to negative feedback.

In what aspects of your life could you benefit from exercising self-compassion?

Effectively respond to Negative Feedback

Navigate your emotions to effectively respond to negative feedback:

- Avoid becoming defensive. Take notes while actively listening.
- Ask for examples to further your understanding.
- Acknowledge what you're feeling. Allow yourself time to let the intensity of your emotions subside before responding.
- Consider other perspectives. Confirm feedback with another reliable source.
- Accept valid feedback and put it in perspective. You are more than your success and setbacks.
- Focus on the future. Choose a thoughtful response and put in the work.

In most cases, it's best to seek negative feedback in a one-on-one setting, in a location that will allow you and the trusted individual to communicate more openly and honestly. Your feedback provider will likely start with some positive comments to provide balance to the negative feedback they will share. This is where emotions can sometimes become intense for most of us.

When we hear something we don't like or we disagree with, our first inclination will be to defend ourselves. It's not easy to hold back when you feel something is being unfairly represented, whether it really is unfair or not. To avoid becoming defensive, actively listen by taking notes and allowing the feedback provider to explain completely without interruption. The time it takes to write and wait for the end of the commentary will go a long way in letting the intensity of your emotions subside.

Rather than immediately dispute what is being said, wait for the provider to finish their comments and then ask for examples to help further your understanding. For example, if the provider states that you tend to isolate yourself from the team when facing deadline pressure, it's fair to ask for an example of when this has occurred. Once the feedback has been provided, asking for examples is a good way to further your understanding, and provide a non-defensive response.

After you've asked your questions, let the feedback provider know that you will take some time to reflect on what they said. As you reflect, acknowledge the emotions that you're feeling. Then allow some time to pass so you can soberly evaluate what was communicated to you. If you feel that some of the feedback was inaccurate, confirming the feedback with another reliable source is a justifiable option. After your evaluation of the feedback is complete, humbly accept the valid negative feedback but put it in perspective! Your identity and your worth is not tied to your performance. Remember that you are so much more than your wins and losses.

Once you've accepted the feedback, focus on the future and leave the mistakes in the past. Learn from your own experience and choose a thoughtful response that truly addresses the feedback you've received. Doing so will move you closer to your goals. Exercising self-compassion throughout this process is the key to successfully navigating your emotions when receiving negative feedback. Don't be too hard on yourself! You are learning and taking the necessary steps to keep developing yourself.

How does exercising self-compassion help you effectively respond to constructive negative feedback?

Do you believe?

So, do you believe that you can achieve your goals? Yes? Well let me dig a little deeper. Do you believe in yourself? Do you believe in your intrinsic value as a person apart from your goals and accomplishments? Do you recognize that you have something to offer this world, even when "they" try to convince you otherwise? Do you believe in your ability to learn, change, and grow? Are you prepared to exercise self-compassion when you fall short of your goals or make a mistake? Are you ready to humble yourself as you receive constructive negative feedback that will aid in your personal development? I've had more than a slice of humble pie and it's cold, soggy, and a bit tart.

If you answered no to any of these questions, you are not alone, so don't be discouraged. Exercise self-compassion and recognize that your journey is just beginning and the growth required to achieve your goals can be extracted from your next challenge. Exercising self-compassion and building a positive self-esteem is a continuous process. As you continue to build healthy and supportive relationships, and as you take on new challenges, accomplishing your goals, small and large, smart and noble, you will build a positive self-esteem and will be able to reject harmful feedback on its face.

Believe in yourself, both who you are today, and who you have the capacity to become.

Don't let anyone convince you otherwise!

A word of warning though. . . . Please don't be the one who gets it twisted and believes that they are the light of the world and can do no wrong. Yes, I'm talking about you, Timmy. My words of encouragement are intended especially for those who doubt their abilities and feel unworthy of caring and supportive relationships. I am blessed to have been raised by parents who loved me and treated me with care. I am blessed to have brothers, sisters, cousins, coworkers, and friends that provide encouragement and support. I am blessed to have a loving wife and two sons who look at me adoringly, letting me know that they appreciate me as much as I appreciate them. All of this helps me view myself positively.

You may experience similar blessings. You may have none of these blessings. You have value and worth just the same. If no one else has ever told you this, let me be the first to tell you emphatically that you have worth and you have something to offer the world. If you already know this, it's on you to pay it forward and spread that love and encouragement to those around you. In chapter 6, we'll do just that. Let's go!

Practice EQ

1. **Apply Consequential Thinking – Key Takeaway #5**
   a. What should be your response to harmful deconstructive feedback?
   b. How should you effectively respond to negative constructive feedback?
   c. Why is it important to exercise self-compassion?
2. Exercise Optimism – Forgive yourself
   a. We've all made mistakes in our life. Everyone will fall short of their goals at one time or another. We sometimes disappoint

ourselves and the people closest too us. But you can find the strength to move forward if you're willing to exercise self-compassion.

i. Write a letter to yourself, acknowledging your mistakes and missteps without making excuses. After your acknowledgements, forgive yourself and positively reaffirm your value and your ability to grow.

Notes

Notes

SIX

Live Inspired!

My Dreams Keep Me Up At Night

My dreams keep me up at night
I lay down and my heart races
There is such anticipation of a finish line I'm afraid I'll never cross
For each dream there is a fear
An alternate nightmare
That my failures bring my sons to tears

I guess restless would describe my heartbeat and my vibe
It's amplified 10 times when I recline
So the pressure that I feel when I lay my head to rest is distress
My heart beating out of my chest
It just wants what's best for you, you, and you
And him and her and you in the back too

Just think of the things we could change if we lead with love and followed up with action instead of a Kanye shrug
So in order to teach a lesson, I pose to you this question...
What is more powerful than fear?
Answer?
The belief that you can be the one to change the feeling in the air

Elements of nitrogen and oxygen
Mixed with vapors of oppression and supremacy
Forms a smog so thick, I'm sick
And George Floyd…
He can't breathe.
That's why I'm so concerned about our legacy

But in my dream, I saw a future where a young'n took a stand and inspired a generation to move beyond second class
Overtook the political system with a multicultural coalition
And promised to protect us all as equal under the law
Walked it, then talked it, conversation started
As God's children grew closer those ugly smog clouds departed!

What a dream! What a thought to think that this could be
What a future, what a world this would be to see
How surreal it is to feel both hope and fear
How exhausting to lie awake at night because you care
And greet the pink sun as it rises time after time
For each dream that you dream there's a bag under your eye

When your vision is God-given and placed in your heart
There is an unrelenting pull telling you to get up and start
Don't you dare turn away. Don't you dare try to hide.
You can try to escape…
But it waits for you at night when you try to close your eyes
I pray, your dreams keep you up at night.

"My dreams keep me up at night" addresses the challenges we face on the way to achieving one's vision. In the poem, I ask "what is more powerful than fear?" Presenting an example of when our thoughts, emotions, and esteem represent internal challenges to one's vision. I also speak about "concern for our legacy," prompted by present-day societal and political discrimination which presents a challenge to different people groups inequitably. No matter who you are, or where you grew up, you will encounter challenges in life. You have your challenges and I certainly have had mine.

Within the couple of years that I've been constructing this *Live Inspired* project, my mother suddenly passed away. My mom and I had a great relationship and we could talk about everything and nothing at the same time. Our last debate before she passed was about whether canned beans were just as healthy as bagged beans. There was no winner. My mom was proud of my poem "What's Real." She grinningly shared it with friends and family. She was thrilled to be featured in the video for my poem "The Design." Today, I couldn't be happier that my mom and dad danced together in that video. I know she would have appreciated my poem "Kerosene" which addresses racial inequities in society.

I miss her dearly, and I will continue to miss her. I miss both of my grandmothers who played a big role in how I was raised. My family and I miss them all dearly. It feels like the grief will never fully pass. My friends who have endured the passing of loved ones for a much longer period of time tell me that I'm right. The feeling of grief may dull over the time, but it never fully disappears. This is one challenge that I am currently dealing with . . . the feeling of longing for the love of those I won't see again in this life.

As a society we've encountered some severe collective challenges as well. The onslaught of COVID-19 has left so many families with a painful feeling of grief which I understand all too well. The racism that has existed for centuries has finally come to the forefront of the nation and the world's consciousness. Hate crimes are on the rise, particularly against those within the Asian community. The struggle to treat immigrant families with compassion and decency continues. We've witnessed a deadly insurrection which resulted in a confederate flag making its way through the U.S. capitol building. Our democracy is being threatened by an open assault on voting rights across most states. The list goes on and on.

The challenges will continue to come. For most of us they have already arrived. But because you've invested in your own development by engaging in this self-study, you are now equipped to address these challenges and choose your responses wisely. This is about control. You can't control the world we live in. We can't control some of the circumstances we live through. We often can't even dictate the emotions that we feel. But with practice, we CAN manage our response. We can use our emotions as information to help us manage our response to challenges we face on the way to achieving meaningful goals. Because you have committed yourself to this study, you've learned how to do just that.

You've learned that To KNOW YOURSELF is to be self-aware. You have learned how to identify what you're feeling and how you may typically react. To GIVE YOURSELF is to have a sense of self-direction. You set a noble goal based on what is meaningful to you and others and you make decisions with this in mind. To CHOOSE YOURSELF is to practice self-management. Knowing what you're feeling and knowing where you're going provides the information you need to help you choose behaviors and responses that will propel you forward and not set you back. Choosing yourself is about understanding that you can navigate your emotions, evaluate your options, and assess the pros and cons of a certain response. Learning all of this, you now have a strong foundation on which to build and practice your EQ skills. I hope you feel encouraged! You have started the process of equipping yourself to overcome the internal and external challenges that you will face on your road of success. Continue seeking opportunities to grow and go forward knowing that your goals are within reach. Do your thing...

Practice EQ - Live Inspired Reflection

Congratulations on investing in yourself and your future! You've undoubtedly learned a lot about yourself and what's important to you. Now it's time to pull together what you've learned and practice self-direction by engaging in self-reflection. But before we get to the work, let's recap some of the key concepts we learned.

> To live inspired means that you are in active pursuit of goals aligned with your purpose.

We are tasked with using our talents to aid us in our purpose. You can find joy where your purpose aligns with a passion. You are within the proximity of your passion whenever you feel energized while engaged in an activity, area of study, or cause that is important to you. If you haven't identified a passion of yours yet, make a decision to get out there and try new things!

To identify potential causes that move you, start by thinking critically about life challenges that affect you and the people you love. Then consider the different ways, big and small, that you may be able to help them and others that may be going through the same thing. Nothing confirms like experience, so engage in that passion and when you have given it your best, grant yourself the space to reassess what it means to you.

Remember, a noble goal is a brief statement of purpose that is intended to help you connect your daily choices with your overarching sense of purpose. As you pursue your noble goal, remember that there are many different pathways on the road of success. Exercise optimism and recognize that you have options! Beyond the traditional pathways we explored, you can become a social media influencer, cryptocurrency miner, or venture capitalist, among other things. Continue to explore even when you feel discouraged by today's challenges.

To progress on the road of success, set specific, measurable, achievable, realistic, and time-oriented (SMART) goals that are aligned with your noble goal. You must be willing to commit to your SMART goals in order to overcome the obstacles you will encounter. Commitment is a mindset that is made real by your actions, so focus your mind, reinforce your messaging, and make strategic moves. Everyone stumbles or falls short of their goals at times. Be patient with yourself and exercise self-compassion on your journey. If you struggle with exercising self-compassion, remember that it is a skill that must be practiced. Exercising compassion in advocacy and service of others will make it easier to be compassionate toward yourself! An added benefit of showing compassion is that because you show compassion to others, those same individuals are likely to do the same for you. It's a beautiful cycle that adds to our collective humanity and has an immensely positive impact in our communities.

I have asked you many questions, but maybe none more impactful than these: Do you believe? Do you believe in your ability to learn and grow? Do you believe you are equipped to effectively respond to feedback? Do you believe that you have something to offer? These are not rhetorical questions. In "My Dreams Keep Me Up At Night," I describe a surreal feeling of "hope and fear." The fear lies in the internal and external challenges that we face. Hope is a byproduct of your belief about yourself and your purpose. If you believe you have a purpose and believe that you can grow to live in it, then you have hope! Hope is "the belief that you can be the one to change the feeling in the air." Hope is the energy that launches you into action when you feel that "unrelenting pull to get up and start." Do you feel that unrelenting pull to just do it? Maybe you do. Maybe, just maybe . . . you're starting to believe that you can accomplish your wildest dreams. To live inspired, you must hold on to this belief for dear life. I encourage you to reaffirm your belief in yourself and your purpose everyday, starting now with your Live Inspired Reflection.

Personal Reflection

In your quest to live inspired, you will need to know where you want to go, why you're going there, how to get there, the people that will join you on the ride, the pit stops you'll need to make, and the resources you'll need for the journey. Fortunately for you, you have already thought about this as you responded to the Key Takeaway from each chapter. It's time to pull it all together and form a plan that will positively affirm your vision of an inspired life. In your reflection you will need to address the following points and include in your response your key takeaways from each chapter:

- A noble goal is a brief and compelling statement about the purpose of your life. What is your noble goal? Describe why this goal is important to you and how you will pursue it.
- Envision the challenges that you may encounter and describe how you will use what you have learned to overcome those challenges.
- Do you believe that you can achieve your goals? Why or why not?

"No Way Is The Way" is one of the Six Seconds learning philosophies. Meaning that experiential learning requires the freedom to be creative. Below are suggested forms of response for your reflection, but feel free to express yourself in a manner that is unique to you.

- Personal essay or short story (600+ words)
- A poem, rap, or song (video or live performance)
- A short film or documentary (4+ minutes)

Nothing to it but to do it! Do your thing, make it your own, and have fun! When you're done, consider sharing your project with friends, family, classmates, coworkers, faith groups, etc. Don't forget me! I would love to hear about how you've grown and what you've learned during this project. You can reach me on most social media platforms by searching @KS4Inspiration.

Summary of Key Takeaways

For your quick reference, here is a summary of the Key Takeaways from each chapter:

1. **Engage Intrinsic Motivation – Key Takeaway #1**
   a. Now that you're in a clearer state of mind. In your personal notes, write down your response to the following questions. If you're not quite ready to answer the questions, write down the emotions that are triggered by each question and consider why you may have that emotional response.
      i. What are your talents?
      ii. What are you passionate about?
      iii. What have your life experiences taught you about your purpose?
      iv. What career or academic pathway would allow you to use your talents within your passion in service of your purpose?
2. **Pursue Noble Goals – Key Takeaway #2**
   a. What is your noble goal?
      i. Develop one concise noble goal that addresses all of the following elements. Extra credit if you can condense it all

into just six words or less. For example, using my definition of success as a starting point, I summarized my noble goal into one easy to remember sentence: "To inspire others to live purposefully."

3. **Pursue Noble Goals – Key Takeaway #3**
   a. Develop a SMART goal based on pursuing a particular career pathway and describe how it is connected to your noble goal.
   b. Develop two to three SMART goals based on actions you can take today to begin exploring a hobby, extracurricular activity, volunteer opportunity, or other career preview opportunity. If you have already identified one of your talents, consider participating in an activity that will strengthen and enhance it. If you've identified a passion of yours, consider participating in a cause or activity that will allow you to sustain that energy and share it with others. Group activities are preferred over individual ones. To accelerate your growth, place yourself around others who will encourage your exploration, challenge you, and nurture your talents.
4. **Exercise Optimism – Key Takeaway #4**
   a. Reflect on one or two of the SMART goals you previously set. When approaching obstacles that threaten your commitment, what actions can you take to:
      i. Focus your mind to remind you of your why and engage intrinsic motivation?
         1. *Ex. Brainstorm with a parent, mentor, or guidance counselor on different strategies or pathways to overcome obstacles.*
         2. *Ex. Make a daily to-do list in order to be present and focus on overcoming today's obstacles.*
      ii. Refine your messaging to exercise optimism?
         1. *Ex. Create a playlist of inspirational and motivational songs.*

2. *Ex. Practice mindfulness or pray daily finding strength in your faith.*

iii. Make strategic moves to promote consistency?

1. *Ex. Share my progress toward my goal with a friend weekly.*
2. *Ex. Limit television/social media usage to an hour per day on the weekdays.*

5. **Apply Consequential Thinking – Key Takeaway #5**
   a. What should be your response to harmful deconstructive feedback?
   b. How should you effectively respond to negative constructive feedback?
   c. Why is it important to exercise self-compassion?

Notes

Notes

ABOUT THE AUTHOR

Kevin Saunders inspires the world to live purposefully by sharing his life experience via motivational and inspirational art. Whether performing his original spoken word poetry, sharing personal stories of life lessons learned, or creating thought-provoking social media content, Kevin values every opportunity to share his art and experiences with others.

Born in Belize City but raised in Yonkers, NY, Kevin made the most of the opportunities this country afforded him. He graduated with an MBA from Pace University and obtained the elusive CPA (Certified Public Accountant) and CFP (Certified Financial Planner) designations while working for Deloitte, a global profressional services firm. More important than his career achievements is his relationship with God, his wife, and the two boys that they raise with the support of a large and loving family. With all the blessings he has received, he has never lost sight of the need to share his experience and knowledge with the community, in hopes that his story can encourage others to live inspired, pursuing meaningful goals aligned with one's purpose.

Kevin is committed to inspiring high school students, college students, and young professionals as a dynamic speaker, facilitator, and performance artist. Through KS4Inspiration, Kevin endeavors to provide inspiration and education to the next generation so that our young people will have the knowledge, discernment, and confidence required to achieve meaningful and impactful goals.

Appendix A

External Resources

www.dosomething.org – For youth-led volunteer opportunities.

www.usa.gov/volunteer – Public service and volunteer opportunities for all ages.

www.hobbyhelp.com - You can find an expansive list of hobbies on the website.

www.handshake.com – For college students seeking jobs and internships.

www.internships.com – For high school, undergraduate, and graduate students seeking jobs and internships.

www.linkedin.com – For students and professionals seeking job and career opportunities.

www.indeed.com – For students and professionals seeking job and career opportunities.

www.fastweb.com – For students seeking college scholarships.

www.scholarships.com – For students seeking college scholarships.

Appendix B - Poems

Crossroad

What do you do when you're at a crossroad and neither road leads to home?
You shutter in fear, stand there and make a decision alone
You pray one road leads to a throne, a crown, an audience, a bow
But what if both roads are despair, a drop, a door that's locked, a hate pot pie, a mistake, a lie...
You stand and ponder, wait a bit longer
Pray for direction, you stay
Correction...
You freeze in panic, your heartbeat is static
It slows, it thumps, you stumble, you front
You pretend to be plotting, you're scared,
You're stopping, you're pensive...

This road isn't for you, that's the truth
Concocted, created, convinced, believed
A lie turned fact, a choice, a pact, YOUR DECISION
So you settle. You have peace. It lasts for a week.
Then you're weak and you're pale, can't sleep, and you sneeze
And you cough, you're diseased, you're blind
You can't see that you've lost what you need to cross and it stings!
This is a life threatening infection
You will either thrive or die
The cure is effort, but the fear of failure is paralyzing
So you lie there in the dark, waiting for the end
But it's a slow death
The loud tick of the clock becomes too much to bear

You CHOOSE resistance, you heighten your senses
Feel your way through the dark, you get up and march.
Momentum builds, you hobble, then step, you SCREAM
you fall, you bleed, you sweat, you cry
You inhale what you thought was your very last breath
Yet...you step...step...step...

Accept Yourself

I am cut from a different cloth
A square on a quilt
Never quite fit in with a squad or a clique
Hated on for a difference in the way that I think
Saw no value in a chain or pink chinchilla mink
I had ambition before I knew that it was fuel for a mission
Headed somewhere fast, the destination was missing

I raised my hand in class to ask and answer the question
They would laugh and smirk, like "Ha! Dude is a nerd!"
Yeah I heard, yeah it hurt, yeah it's words, yeah i cared,
Yeah I splurged on some Avirex, Tims, Girbauds
Got fresh to get them off my neck, next step was get the girls
Now I'm cool cause I'm "ghetto" but I couldn't drop the nerd…

I guess fitting in wasn't meant to be
When I think about it, even my tormentors saw something different in me
It took me long enough, but now I finally see
I was gifted with a drive for the mission
Uniquely designed for a path less traveled
So I smash your gavel if you judge my craft

Foolishness says to be one in a crowd
But the smart money, is to be one in a thou
You are gifted! Don't be afraid to announce it
With all the naysayers in the world trying to denounce it
You are more than enough, just accept yourself
And realize nothing is in your way...except yourself
When you hit the roadblock, accept some help
When you climb that mountain, lift someone else
That's the greatest law, right? To love thy neighbor?
Even if that neighbor...is a hater

My Dreams Keep Me Up At Night

My dreams keep me up at night
I lay down and my heart races
There is such anticipation of a finish line I'm afraid I'll never cross
For each dream there is a fear
An alternate nightmare
That my failures bring my sons to tears

I guess restless would describe my heartbeat and my vibe
It's amplified 10 times when I recline
So the pressure that I feel when I lay my head to rest is distress
My heart beating out of my chest
It just wants what's best for you, you, and you
And him and her and you in the back too

Just think of the things we could change if we lead with love and followed up with action instead of a Kanye shrug
So in order to teach a lesson, I pose to you this question...
What is more powerful than fear?
Answer?
The belief that you can be the one to change the feeling in the air

Elements of nitrogen and oxygen
Mixed with vapors of oppression and supremacy
Forms a smog so thick, I'm sick
And George Floyd…
He can't breathe.
That's why I'm so concerned about our legacy

But in my dream, I saw a future where a young'n took a stand and inspired a generation to move beyond second class
Overtook the political system with a multicultural coalition
And promised to protect us all as equal under the law
Walked it, then talked it, conversation started
As God's children grew closer those ugly smog clouds departed!

What a dream! What a thought to think that this could be
What a future, what a world this would be to see
How surreal it is to feel both hope and fear
How exhausting to lie awake at night because you care
And greet the pink sun as it rises time after time
For each dream that you dream there's a bag under your eye

When your vision is God-given and placed in your heart
There is an unrelenting pull telling you to get up and start
Don't you dare turn away. Don't you dare try to hide.
You can try to escape…
But it waits for you at night when you try to close your eyes
I pray, your dreams keep you up at night.

Acknowledgements

Thank God! I was only able to endure the long process of bringing this study to life because Jesus gave his life for me. I pray this work blesses all who read it and that it is received with the love and enthusiasm with which it was crafted.

Thank you Jenn. You are everything. Love you for life.

Thank you Carmen, for your editing contributions.

Thank you Albatross Book Co., for a beautiful book design.

Thank you Farzana for the initial logo design.

Thank you Chris and Heriberta for your insights as educators. Our youth are lucky to have you both.

Thank you Josh, Cherilyn, Marilynn, Lynette, Jim, Kelli, Lize, Dr. Liza, and the entire Six Seconds team for lending your wisdom and insight to this work.

Shout to my dad, Ma Lewis, Pop Lewis, my brothers and sisters and all of my family and friends for your love and support.

One time for my boys, my niece, nephews, godchildren, and cousins. I pray you all LIVE INSPIRED!

Endnotes

1 *Dictionary.com*, s.v. "Passion," accessed https://www.dictionary.com/browse/passion?s=t

2 Finley, Taryn, "12-Year-Old Marley Dias To Publish Activism Guide For Kids And Teens," Black Voices, *Huffpost*, February 14, 2017, https://www.huffpost.com/entry/marley-dias-book-activism_n_58a32433e4b094a129ef1a33

3 *Dictionary.com*, s.v. "Purpose," accessed https://www.dictionary.com/browse/purpose

4 Hackett, Conrad, and David McClendon, "Christians remain world's largest religious group, but they are declining in Europe," *Pew Research Center*, April 5, 2017, https://www.theguardian.com/news/2018/aug/27/religion-why-is-faith-growing-and-what-happens-next and https://www.pewresearch.org/fact-tank/2017/04/05/christians-remain-worlds-largest-religious-group-but-they-are-declining-in-europe/

5 Cherry, Kendra, "Differences of Extrinsic and Intrinsic Motivation," Psychology, *Verywell Mind*, January 15, 2020, https://www.verywellmind.com/differences-between-extrinsic-and-intrinsic-motivation-2795384

6 *Dictionary.com*, s.v. "Talent," accessed https://www.dictionary.com/browse/talent

7 Newsweek Special Edition, "Michael Jordan Didn't Make Varsity–At First," Culture, *Newsweek*, October 17, 2015, www.newsweek.com/missing-cut-382954

8 Davis, Daphne M., Jeffery A. Hayes. "What are the benefits of mindfulness?" *American Psychological Association* 43, no. 7 (July/August 2012): 64, https://www.apa.org/monitor/2012/07-08/ce-corner

9 *Lexico*, s.v. "Success," accessed https://www.lexico.com/en/definition/success

10 21 Savage, "Bank Account," YouTube video, July 6, 2017, https://www.youtube.com/watch?v=sV2t3tW_JTQ

11 "What Is Nike's Mission?" Nike, accessed https://www.nike.com/help/a/nikeinc-mission

12 "Core Values" Patagonia, accessed https://www.patagonia.com/core-values/

13 "About Tesla" Tesla, accessed https://www.tesla.com/about

14 "Mission & Values" American Red Cross, accessed https://www.redcross.org/about-us/who-we-are/mission-and-values.html

15 Millar, Michael, "Pursue Noble Goals in the Six Seconds Model of EQ," *Six Seconds: The Emotional Intelligence Network* (August 29, 2017), https://www.6seconds.org/2017/08/29/pursue-noble-goals/

16 Millar, "Pursue Noble Goals," https://www.6seconds.org/2017/08/29/pursue-noble-goals/

17 Dalai Lama, Desmond Tutu, and Douglas Carlton Abrams. *The Book of Joy: Lasting Happiness in a Changing World*, (New York: Penguin Random House, 2016).

18 Doran, George T.,"There's a S.M.A.R.T. way to write management's goals and objectives," *Management Review* 70, no. 11 (1981): 35–36, PDF file, https://community.mis.temple.edu/mis0855002fall2015/files/2015/10/S.M.A.R.T-Way-Management-Review.pdf

19 https://www.dominican.edu/academics/lae/undergraduate-programs/psych/faculty/assets-gail-matthews/researchsummary2.pdf

20 "Occupation Finder: Occupational Outlook Handbook," U.S. Bureau of Labor Statistics, last modified April 9, 2021, https://www.bls.gov/ooh/occupation-finder.htm?pay=&education=&training=&newjobs=&growth=&submit=GO

21 Hayes, Adam, "Entrepreneurs," Business Essentials, *Investopia*, February 26, 2021, https://www.investopedia.com/terms/e/entrepreneur.asp

22 Gustafson, Katherine, "What Percentage of Businesses Fail and How to Improve Your Chances of Success," *LendingTree*, August 7, 2020, https://www.lendingtree.com/business/small/failure-rate/#:~:text=According%20to%20data%20from%20the,failure%20rates%20are%20fairly%20consistent

23 "The Top 20 Reasons Startups Fail," Research Briefs, *CB Insights*, November 6, 2019, https://www.cbinsights.com/research/startup-failure-reasons-top/

24 "10 steps to start your business," *U.S. Small Business Administration*, accessed https://www.sba.gov/business-guide/10-steps-start-your-business

25 *Dictionary.com*, s.v. "Volunteer," accessed https://www.dictionary.com/browse/volunteer

26 Biography, "Mahatma Gandhi," *Biography*, April 27, 2017, https://www.biography.com/activist/mahatma-gandhi

27 Goalcast, "Top 20 Most Famous and Inspiring Mahatma Gandhi Quotes," *Goalcast*, March 20, 2017, https://www.goalcast.com/2017/03/20/top-20-inspiring-mahatma-gandhi-quotes/

28 HelpGuide, "Volunteering and its Surprising Benefits," *HelpGuide.org*, accessed https://www.helpguide.org/articles/healthy-living/volunteering-and-its-surprising-benefits.htm

29 *Collins Dictionary online*, s.v. "Hobby," accessed https://www.collinsdictionary.com/us/dictionary/english/hobby

30 "Walt's Quotes," *Walt Disney Archives* (blog), *The Official Disney Fan Club*, accessed https://d23.com/section/walt-disney-archives/walts-quotes/

31 *Wikipedia,* s.v. "Extracurricular activity," accessed https://en.wikipedia.org/wiki/Extracurricular_activity

32 *YourDictionary.com*, "Recreational activities," accessed https://www.yourdictionary.com/recreational-activities

33 *New Oxford American Dictionary*, s.v. "Internship," accessed https://www.google.com/search?q=define+internship&rlz=1C1GCEB_enUS841US841&oq=define+in&aqs=chrome.0.69i59l3j69i57j0l4.2339j0j4&sourceid=chrome&ie=UTF-8

34 Cairns, Hilary, "What is Job Shadowing?" *College Raptor*, June 19, 2020, https://www.collegeraptor.com/explore-careers/articles/careers-internships/what-is-job-shadowing/

35 Oshinkale, Yetunde, "Definition of Mentorship: What is a Mentor and Do You Need One?" *West Advisor* (blog), *World Education Services*, September 18, 2019, https://www.wes.org/advisor-blog/definition-of-mentorship/

36 *Vocabulary.com*, s.v. "Commitment," accessed https://www.vocabulary.com/dictionary/commitment

37 Baer, Drake, "Science Says You Should Do Your Most Important Work First Thing in The Morning," Business Insider, *ScienceAlert*, April 30, 2015, https://www.sciencealert.com/science-says-you-should-do-your-most-important-work-first-thing-in-the-morning

38 *Merriam-Webster.com*, s.v. "Habit," accessed https://www.merriam-webster.com/dictionary/habit

39 Dean, Signe, "Here's How Long It Really Takes to Break a Habit, According to Science," Humans, *ScienceAlert*, June 9, 2018, https://www.sciencealert.com/how-long-it-takes-to-break-a-habit-according-to-science

40 Freedman, Joshua, *Hijacking*, PDF file, n.d, http://admin.6seconds.org/wp-content/uploads/2014/01/Hijacking.pdf

41 Stagnor, Charles, "The Feeling Self: Self-Esteem," in *Principles of Social Psychology*, adapted by Rajiv Jhangiani, and Hammond Tarry, BCcampus Open Education, 2014, https://opentextbc.ca/socialpsychology/chapter/the-feeling-

self-self-esteem/#:~:text=Self%2Desteem%20refers%20to%20the,that%20others%20view%20us%20positively

42 Grant, Heidi, "To Succeed, Forget Self-Esteem," Managing Yourself, *Harvard Business Review*, September 20, 2012, https://hbr.org/2012/09/to-succeed-forget-self-esteem

43 Breines, Juliana G., and Serena Chen, "Self-Compassion Increases Self-Improvement Motivation," in Personality and Social Psychology Bulletin, PDF file, *SAGE Publications Inc*, May 29, 2012, doi: 10.1177/0146167212445599 https://self-compassion.org/wp-content/uploads/publications/selfimp.motivation.pdf

44 Sime, Carley, "Why Self-Compassion Beats Self-Esteem," Leadership Strategy, *Forbes*, April 20,2019, https://www.forbes.com/sites/carleysime/2019/04/30/why-self-compassion-beats-self-esteem/#6133f15e5c15

45 Dweck, Carol, "What Having a 'Growth Mindset' Actually Means," Managing Yourself, *Harvard Business Review*, January 13, 2016, https://hbr.org/2016/01/what-having-a-growth-mindset-actually-means

Made in the USA
Middletown, DE
28 September 2022